From Chris Meyer
xmas 1991

From Chris Meyer
xmas 1991

ROCHESTER

"Partners in Progress" by Kay Calvin
Produced in cooperation with the
Rochester Area Chamber of Commerce

Windsor Publications, Inc.
Northridge, California

ROCHESTER

City of the Prairie

Harriet W. Hodgson

Windsor Publications, Inc.—History Books Division
Managing Editor: Karen Story
Design Director: Alexander D'Anca
Staff for *Rochester: City of the Prairie*
Manuscript Editor: Doreen Nakakihara
Photo Editor: Loren Prostano
Editor, Corporate Biographies: Brenda Berryhill
Production Editor, Corporate Biographies: Una
    FitzSimons
Editorial Assistants: Kim Kievman, Michael
    Nugwynne, Kathy B. Peyser, Priscilla Solis,
    Theresa J. Solis
Publisher's Representative, Corporate Biographies:
    John Swedberg
Designer: Tanya Maiboroda
Layout Artist: Robaire Ream
Production Assistant: Bonnie Felt
Layout Artist, Corporate Biographies: Mari
    Catherine Preimesberger

Library of Congress Cataloging-in-Publication Data
Hodgson, Harriet W.
Rochester : city of the prairie.
Bibliography: p. 132
Includes index.
1. Rochester (Minn.)—Description—Views. 3.
    Rochester (Minn.)— Industries.
I. Title.
F614.R6H63   1989   977.6'155   88-37851
ISBN 0-89781-304-9

Windsor Publications, Inc.
Elliot Martin, Chairman of the Board
James L. Fish III, Chief Operating Officer
Michele Sylvestro, Vice President / Sales-Marketing

CONTENTS

PREFACE

I first visited Rochester in the summer of 1955, flying out from Long Island to visit my fiancé's family. In preparation for the trip I read Helen Clapesattle's brilliant biography, *The Doctors Mayo*. Although the biography provided me with factual information about the Mayo Clinic and Rochester, it didn't prepare me for the sight of the city.

The trip was long, tiring, and frightening for a 19-year-old who hadn't traveled before. As we took off from Madison I gazed out the window at the landscape below. Through scudding clouds I saw a patchwork of farms stitched together by straight, rural roads that ran along section lines, and I saw winding streams that glistened in the fading sunlight. Pristine farmhouses stood shielded by tall windbreaks of poplar and pine.

As the plane banked for landing, Rochester suddenly came into view, a bona fide city with skyscrapers, water towers, church spires, housing developments, and green parklands. The city seemed to spring from nowhere. An education major in college, I was reminded of the reading-readiness activity which directed children to "mark the one that doesn't belong." To me, Rochester didn't belong. It was a mismatch. What was a city doing in the midst of the prairie?

This history answers that question. I have approached the book from a topical perspective, rather than a chronological one. Each chapter focuses on a broad topic, starting with the past and progressing toward the future. My research incorporated a variety of sources: legal documents, cookbooks, textbooks, pamphlets, handbills, private correspondence, and personal interviews.

Taping interviews with long-term residents proved to be a project in itself. I realized I couldn't interview every person who contacted me and still meet publication deadlines. Consequently, I decided to limit interviews to two per chapter and started a log of potential interview subjects. All tape-recorded interviews have been donated to the Oral Archives, Olmsted County Historical Society.

This book would not exist without the cooperation of the Olmsted County Historical Society. I am deeply indebted to its volunteers and staff, particularly Beverly Hermes, Librarian/Archivist. Her patience and unfailing humor sustained me throughout months of research. Most of the black-and-white photographs are from the society's splendid files. Many photographs are published here for the first time.

Brad R. Piens, Olmsted County Historical Society photographer, has done a meticulous job of photographing artifacts, advertisements, legal documents, and tintypes. No request was too large, no request was too small, no request was too challenging—all received his careful attention. His work adds a special quality and dimension to this history.

All color photographs, with the exception of the 1874 lithograph of Rochester, are the work of Gary Koenig, a local photographer who worked for months to record the shapes of Rochester on film. His photographic essay not only enhances the text, it captures the dynamic spirit of a city on the move.

I am deeply indebted to Clark Nelson, Mayo Clinic Archivist, for sharing historical photographs and keen personal insights, and to Sister Lauren, St. Marys Archivist, for resources pertaining to the founding of the hospital. Lastly, I am indebted to Robert Retzlaff, Managing Editor of the *Rochester Post-Bulletin,* for allowing me to use newspaper photographs. Bob also deserves a special award for answering Monday morning phone calls with cheerful acumen.

From the beginning, the people of

Rochester embraced this project. There were times when I received as many as four to five calls a day, testimony to public interest. The calls yielded practical leads, information, family photos, and new friendships. Since it is impossible to thank each of you personally, I thank you here.

Your ancestors built this community, your work keeps it going, your children and grandchildren determine its destiny. So I dedicate this history to all Rochester pioneers—past, present, and future. This is your story.

Fishing near the Lake Zumbro dam provides the perfect ending to a sultry summer day. Photo by Gary Koenig

Benjamin Bear and his wife, Maria, were two of Rochester's first settlers. They came to Minnesota via Ohio, Indiana, and Iowa. The Bears had 11 children, 23 grandchildren, and 24 great-grandchildren. After working in the hot sun, Benjamin Bear developed heart trouble and died on August 28, 1902, at age 82. The Olmsted County Democrat said, "In his death, the community loses a good neighbor, and an honest, upright citizen." Courtesy, Olmsted County Historical Society

1

FROM SIOUX TO SODBUSTERS

Three decades after the founding of Rochester, the Board of Trade published a 66-page pamphlet about the city. As was popular at the time, the pamphlet had a lengthy title: *Olmsted County, Minnesota, and Its Advantages of Soil, Climate and Location, with Rochester as a Most Favorable Point for Manufacturing.*

The pamphlet described Rochester's rich farming soil, high crop yield, quality of life, and growth potential. Its text boasted about the nutritious grasses for grazing, clear streams stocked with speckled trout, convenient railroad branch lines, and favorable climate with abundant yearly rainfall. Rochester was touted as the garden spot of the state: "We have smooth roads, little snow, seldom such winter thaws as leave you to wallow in the mud; every day favors outdoor work. Steady dry cold is useful in removing the old year's growth of vegetation without malarious results; and tramps and horse-thieves leave us when they cannot 'lie out.'"

The pamphlet concluded with a list of reasons why businesses should move to Rochester and Olmsted County. Reason number 20 invoked mother love and was printed in capital letters: "BECAUSE IT IS. That is our mother's reason." Publication date of the pamphlet was 1884, remarkable considering Rochester was nonexistent just 30 years before. In this short time span Rochester had progressed from a fledgling village to a bustling city.

Minnesota became the 32nd state on May 11, 1858. Complying with the rules of statehood, Minnesota had adopted a constitution by popular vote, elected state officials, and documented population via census. The first state census, taken in 1850, credits St. Paul with 1,112 residents. Only 80 miles to the southeast the fu-

The "Father of Rochester," George Head, was the first settler to stake his claim, in July 1854. He attempted to take land previously claimed by Smith & Company. Payment of $3,600 to the partners of Smith & Co. resolved the dispute. This energetic pioneer served as deputy sheriff, worked as a baker, and also dabbled in real estate. Courtesy, Olmsted County Historical Society

Facing page: Henrietta Head, wife of George Head, was the first white woman to settle in Rochester. Mrs. Head supposedly led the parade, riding sidesaddle, dragging a massive log through the brush to clear land for Broadway. She married George Head at age 17, and died at age 42. Following her death, George Head married her sister, Sophia. Courtesy, Olmsted County Historical Society

ture site of Rochester was still a tangled wilderness.

Minnesota had high expectations for its new status. Explained Theodore Blegen, author of *Minnesota: A History of the State,* "Statehood, it was believed, would bring better times, attract immigrants, invite capital, and open the way to prosperity." This prediction turned out to be true in Rochester, which, from its founding, attracted immigrants and venture capital.

Confusion exists as to who first discovered the region. One account speculates it was Thomas Simpson, a government land surveyor from Winona, whereas another account reports it was a missionary priest. However, all historians seem to agree on the spectacular beauty of the landscape, described by one as a second Eden.

When first discovered, most of what became Olmsted County was prairie. The prairie grasses stood taller than a human, so tall they reached the waist of a rider on horseback. Where grasses thinned, ground cover began, blanketing the land with wild plum, leadplant, chokecherry,

wild cherry, black cherry, ninebark, wild rose, raspberry, and blackberry bushes. Poison sumac, poison ivy, prickly ash, and nettles also grew in this "Eden." Twenty-five varieties of trees, including jack oak, basswood, sugar maple, butternut, hickory, oak, and coarsely toothed aspen, grew along rolling hillsides and flat floodplains.

Trees grew thickest along riverbanks, particularly along the Zumbro River, which Indians called the River of Obstructions. The French name for the river was *Rivière des Embarras,* which means "river of embarrassment" or "obstruction," probably named so because of the logjams, floating debris, and beaver dams which hindered the river's natural flow. Zumbro was an English approximation of the French name, according to Thomas Waters, author of *The Streams and Rivers of Minnesota.*

George Head was first to stake his claim in July 1854. The Heads, two brothers and their father, came from Wisconsin looking for land. Of the thousands of acres of land between here and the Pacific Ocean, they chose a site previously claimed by Smith & Company and attempted claim jumping. As the Heads began to demolish the cabin that stood on the site, E.S. Smith came upon them. Smith angrily drew his revolver, took menacing aim, and frightened them off. Money finally resolved the dispute, and the claim reverted to the Heads.

George Head spent the summer building a shanty (slang for cabin) 12 feet by 24 feet in dimensions. Head's shanty was made of rough-hewn logs and had a sod roof of bleached prairie grasses. George Head whittled window sashes with his pocket knife and installed oiled-paper panes in the window frames. Because of a lack of materials, or time, or maybe both, a blanket was used as a cabin door, scant protection against the wolves which settlers heard howling at night.

That summer Head somehow found time to build a second shanty, which he subsequently sold to Asa Lesuer. Lesuer converted the cabin into a hotel known as

Head's Tavern. Because the hotel was so small, barely larger than the original Head cabin, it always seemed to be packed wall-to-wall with guests. Head's Tavern was also a good place to get a meal, serving "imported" food from Iowa.

Head named the settlement Rochester after Rochester, New York, which he had visited two years earlier. As the settlement grew, a main street was cleared by hitching a huge tree trunk behind a team of oxen and dragging the log horizontally through the brush. Reflecting the lofty dreams of these early settlers, the street was named Broadway.

Although life on the prairie was not as wild as depicted in Western movies, it was a challenging and sometimes lawless existence. Since the unsurveyed land was free, claim jumping was a common practice. Many a man returned from filing his claim, buying provisions, and gathering his family, only to find strangers living on his land. To curb this practice the Regulators, a committee of concerned locals who sought to enforce legal land claims, was founded.

With the help of brawny settlers, Head built a bridge across the Zumbro River. Three 30-foot stringers, each about three feet above water, provided support for the ambitious project. Poles were laid across the stringers, then covered with layers of hay and sod. Stones, laboriously gathered from the river, formed the final bridge surface and also weighted the structure.

News of the settlement, perhaps exaggerated, spread by word of mouth and print. *The History of Olmsted County, Minnesota* described the broad prairies and charming woodlands which, "at the magic touch of the husbandman's labor and skill," were converted from wilderness into crop-bearing farms.

Settlers poured into Rochester from Wisconsin, Ohio, Indiana, Vermont, New York, and New Jersey. During a single month, July 1855, over 1,000 people immigrated to Minnesota from other states. And immigrants came from other coun-

tries, such as Germany, Scotland, Ireland, England, Norway, and Sweden. Soon dozens of shanties dotted riverbanks, a building practice which proved to be dangerous.

On August 11, 1857, Bear Creek and the Zumbro River flooded. Bridges across

In 1879 the J.M. Cole Flouring Mill was erected. The mill was 48 feet by 76 feet in dimension, stood 75 feet high, and could turn out 200 barrels of flour every 24 hours. Twelve men were employed at the mill. Courtesy, Olmsted County Historical Society

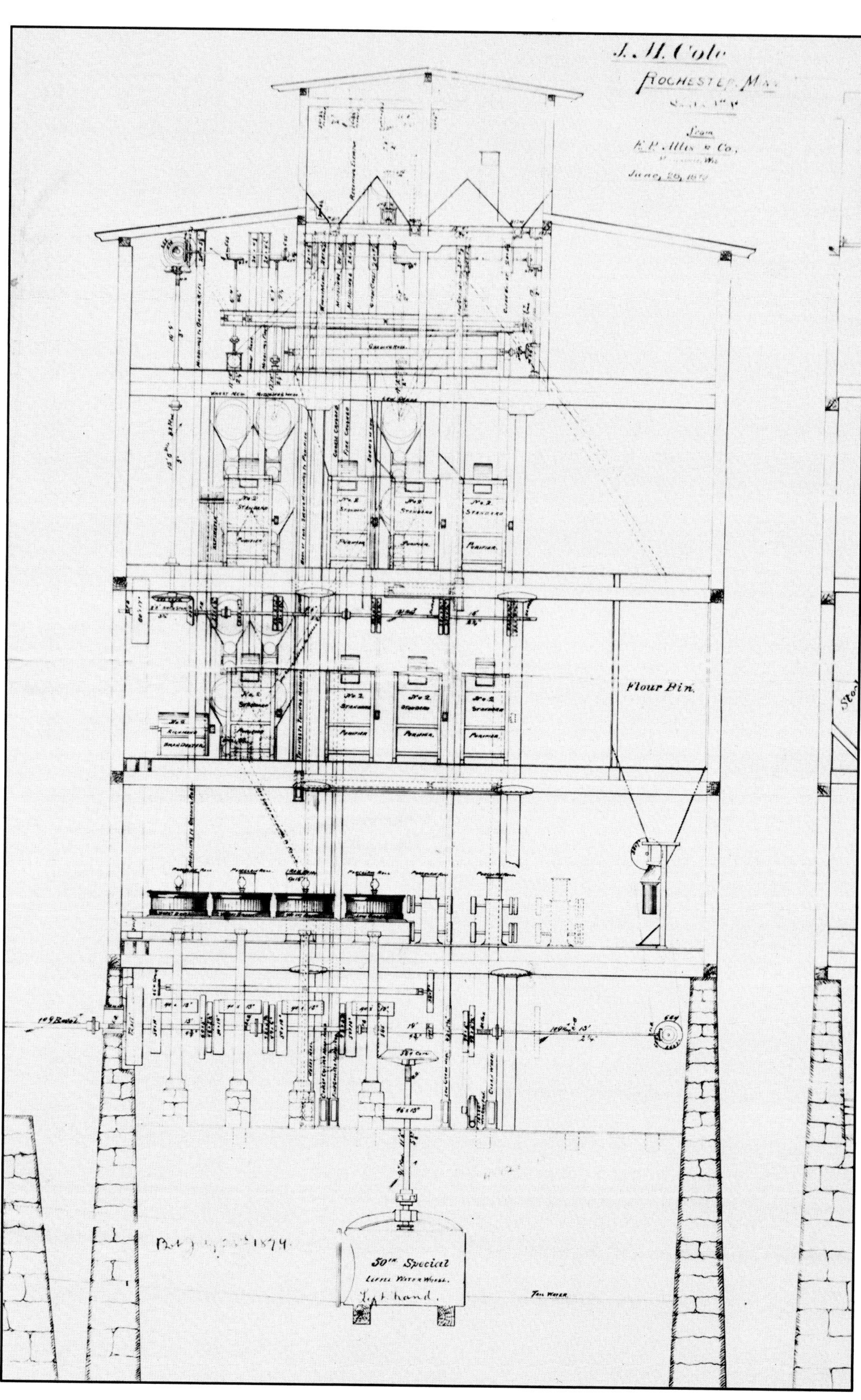

both rivers were swept away in the swirling, turbulent waters. There was one fatality: Nathan Robbins, a young settler, drowned when he tried to swim across the racing waters above Zumbro Falls. Floodwaters rose so swiftly that the settlers could only save themselves, while their shanties swept downriver with bobbing bridge timbers.

Yet abundant rainfall, averaging 7.49 inches during the spring months, was one reason settlers flocked to Rochester. This rainfall, together with a deep layer of rich, black loam, made prairie land ideal for farming. Topsoil varied in depth from one and a half to two and a half feet. Subsistence crops were planted first: potatoes, carrots, onions, and cabbage, followed by wheat and other grains. Farmers were ecstatic at their crop yields, said to be the highest in the known world. Farsighted entrepreneurs became aware of the rapidly growing community and decided to invest in it.

In the spring of 1864 the Boston Company began construction of a four-story flour mill with a 65-foot grain elevator. J.M. Cole bought the mill seven years later and named it after himself. Business was good until floodwaters again rose in 1866, damaging both mill house and waterwheel. When the waters subsided Cole had the mill's height raised by six feet, underpinning the foundation with 100 cords of stone. A new waterwheel was also installed.

Four rivers meandered across the landscape: the Zumbro River, Silver Creek, Cascade Creek, and Bear Creek. Contrary to public opinion, Bear Creek (also spelled Bär, Bair, and Baier) was not named after the animal but after an early Eyota settler, Benjamin Franklin Bear. He built his cabin beside Bear Creek and used its icy waters to store milk and butter. Indians often wandered about the cabin, peeking in windows or walking inside to ask for sugar.

These friendly Indians, primarily Sioux, with some Winnebago, were the first inhabitants of the area. "Prior to 1849 only the trapper, the trader and adventurer dared to face the wilderness, for even as late as 1856 the Indian still ruled the prairies and the stillness of the forests," wrote Ernest Schlitgus. Under the Treaty of Traverse des Sioux, the United States purchased land rights to 20 million acres of Indian land. In 1865 roughly 200 Sioux were camped near Cole's Mill, where they remained for six weeks—well into winter.

During this time, three Indian men and one Indian woman died from a disease some thought was smallpox because of the pustules which appeared on the Indians' skin. Muzomoney, the Sioux physician, believed the woman's death was caused by a bee she had accidentally ingested along with wild honey. The Indians hired two white settlers to bury their dead—perhaps because they feared reinfection. But burial of the deceased did not halt the spread of the dis-

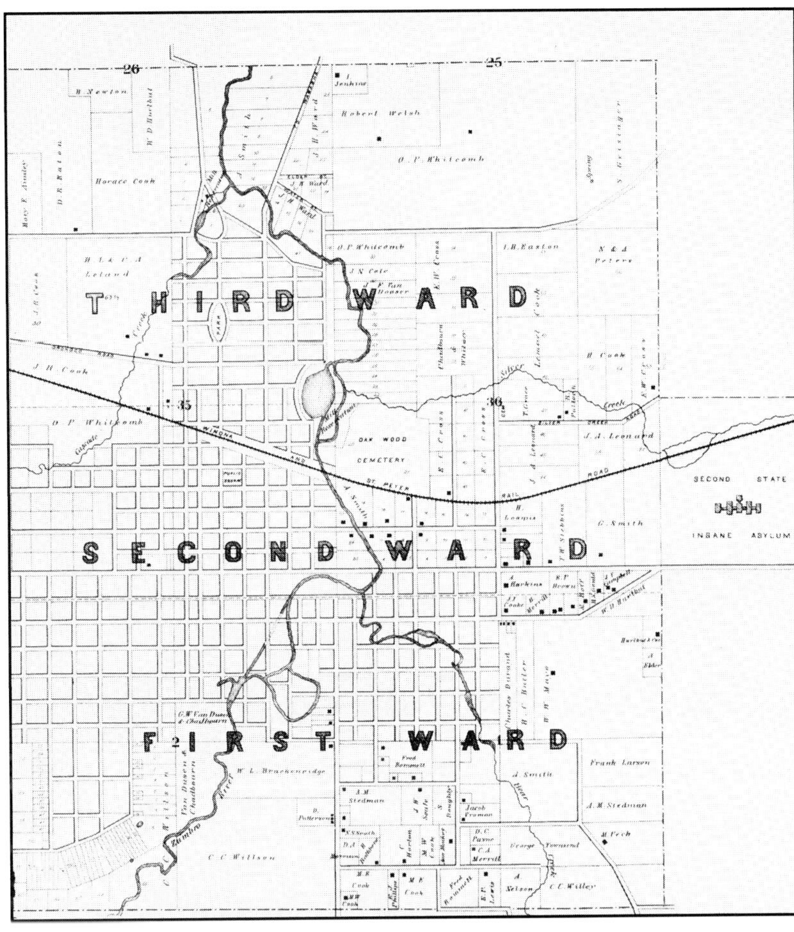

This map from the 1878 Plat Book of Olmsted County clearly illustrates the four rivers: Zumbro River, Bear Creek, Silver Creek, and Cascade Creek, which converge in Rochester. The location of these rivers had contributed to the city's long-term flooding problems. However, tributaries of the Zumbro River, which comprise a watershed of 1,428 miles in Minnesota, provide countless canoeing opportunities for tourists and residents. Courtesy, Dr. and Mrs. C. John Hodgson

ease. Two more Indians died, as well as a young chieftain who expired from wounds inflicted by his pony.

Disheartened, the Sioux broke camp and moved south to another area. The tribe believed they had escaped the mysterious disease until a young female named Winona became ill. They quarantined Winona in a teepee for two days, where she lay—if accounts can be believed—without food or water. Although not fully recovered, Winona walked to the nearby home of James Bucklin, who nursed her back to health.

In return the grateful Winona presented Bucklin with two gifts: a hunting knife and a pair of moccasins. Her gifts

mark the end of the Sioux settlement in Rochester, for when spring arrived no Sioux could be found. They had vanished completely, perhaps moving on to the Dakota Territory.

Besides the hazards of weather, Rochester pioneers contended with stabbings, bank robberies, and outlaw gangs. Staunch settlers were not averse to hiring detectives to help maintain law and order. A Chicago detective was hired to track down one murder suspect, George Staley. Doggedly the detective traced the fugitive to a lumber camp in Wisconsin. Lawmen raided the camp around three in the morning and asked the sleeping lumberjacks to show their faces. Staley hid his

face beneath a blanket. The detective, who had a picture of the suspect, wasted neither time nor words. "Get up, I want you," he reportedly said before returning the suspect to Rochester.

Missionaries followed the twisting path of the Mississippi River and made their way inland to Rochester. They preached to anyone—anywhere. A Methodist minister was the first clergyman to arrive, in 1856, and he conducted services in John Crabb's log cabin. Two years later a Baptist minister arrived and with six energetic members built the first church, a wooden structure completed in 1858. Baptisms were performed in the Zumbro River behind the church.

Other clergymen came, including Episcopal, Catholic, Presbyterian, Lutheran, and Congregational. The Congregational minister, an adaptable chap, preached Sunday sermons in Head's Tavern for two months. The Universalist Society started its church in 1860 with 40 members. The congregation, however, was unable to sustain membership when many of its male members enlisted in the Union army at the start of the Civil War. Six years later the church resurged, its members now calling themselves "friends of progress."

Small businesses sprang up quickly to support village life. J.D. Jenkins opened his general store in a log cabin in 1855, stocking it with wet and dry goods. Jenkins' store was instantly popular, perhaps because of the cask of gin he kept on reserve, which was the first liquor in Rochester. W.H. Mitchell reported, in his *History of the County of Olmsted*, "the cask was never empty, and never would be empty, so long as water flowed in the Zumbro."

A smithy opened for business in 1856, locating his shop on the banks of the Zumbro. Five years later the business moved to Broadway, expanding its stock to include boots and lace. Ten years later Scandinavian settlers opened Rochester's first bakery. The bakery, a boon to hardworking, hungry residents, sold fresh-baked bread, cakes, pies, biscuits, rolls, and buns. On Zumbro Street the Success Wash-

ing Machine Company opened its doors for business. Demand for the contraptions was so high that the manufacturer was forced to advertise: "all orders filled in the order in which they are given."

Women welcomed any labor-saving device. They not only cared for their families but worked beside their husbands planting crops and cooked for large threshing crews at harvest time. Early in its history the state of Minnesota published pamphlets and books to aid housewives. One helpful guide, *Buckeye Cookery, with Hints on Practical Housekeeping,* was an all-purpose resource named after the publisher. This 1883 cookbook was used by many Rochester housewives. "No sloven can make good butter," admonished the authors. The book contained recipes for any-

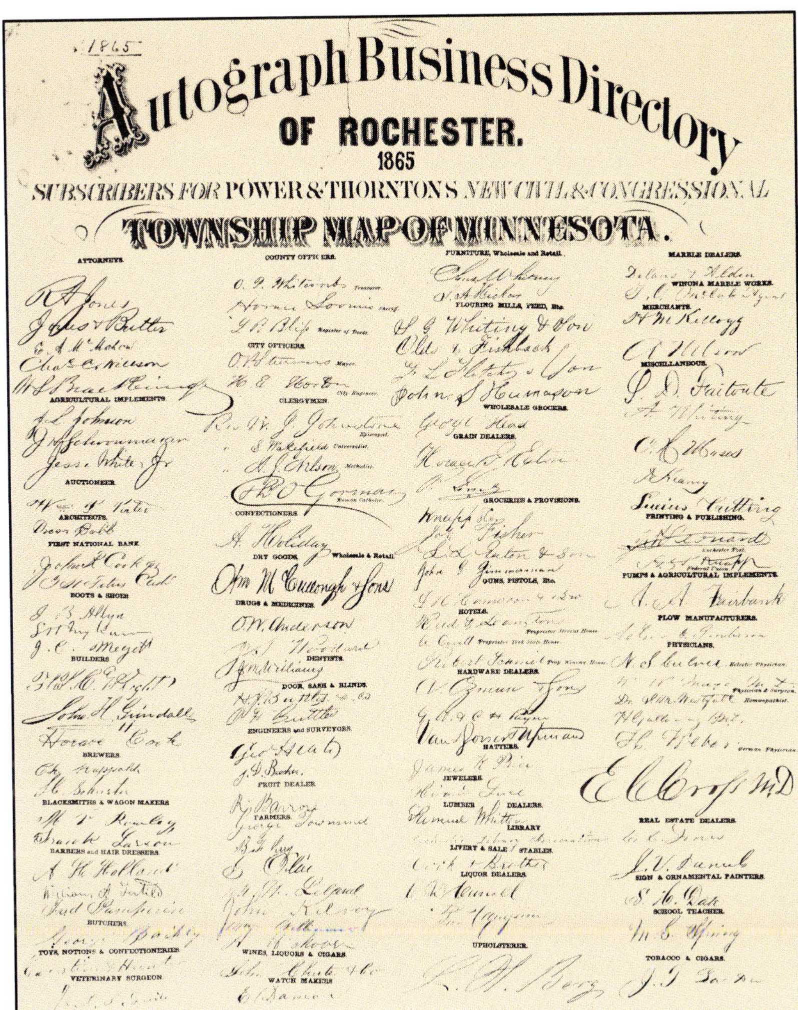

Rochester businessmen didn't wait for business to come their way. They were aggressive marketeers, and published an Autograph Business Directory in 1865. Courtesy, Olmsted County Historical Society

HOUSEKEEPER COOK BOOK.

RACK FOR SPICE.—The cut represents a neat rack in which is set small cans containing spices. The handle is a convenience, and the rack may be kept close at hand while cakes are made, and when the work is done set away on a shelf or in a cupboard until needed again.

RACK FOR TOAST.—Toast, to be palatable or healthful, must be dry and crisp, and to keep it in this condition, after toasting, the slices must be kept apart, to prevent their gathering moisture and becoming tough. The English, who are very fond of dry toast, place it upon the table in a toast rack, which preserves its quality and crispness. Silver racks are costly, and out of the reach of the masses, but the rack here represented is made of white wire, and is as neat and clean as silver, and very cheap. In a large family two will be required, as the delicious quality of the toast prepared in this way creates a lively demand for it.

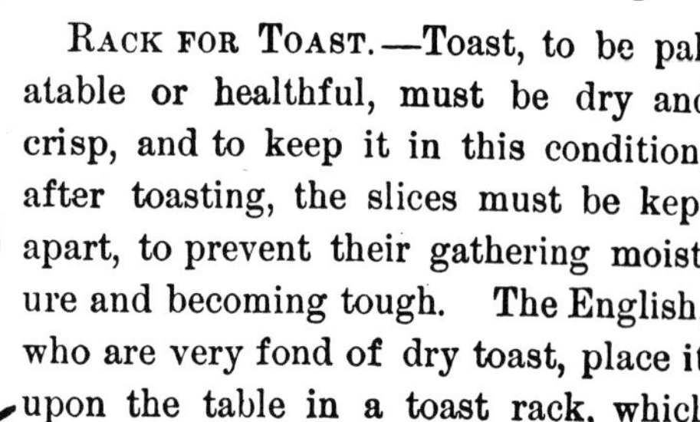

ROASTING PAN.—Every kitchen should be supplied with a self-basting pan, as the flavor and juiciness of meats thus cooked is much better preserved than in an open pan.

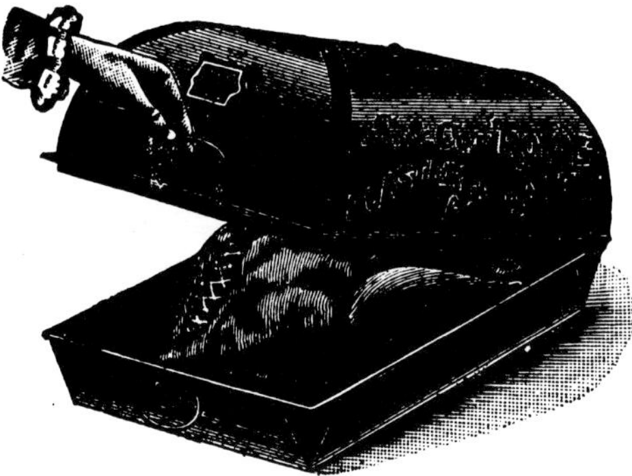

STRAINER.—This strainer has an extension wire frame which is made to rest on the top of a

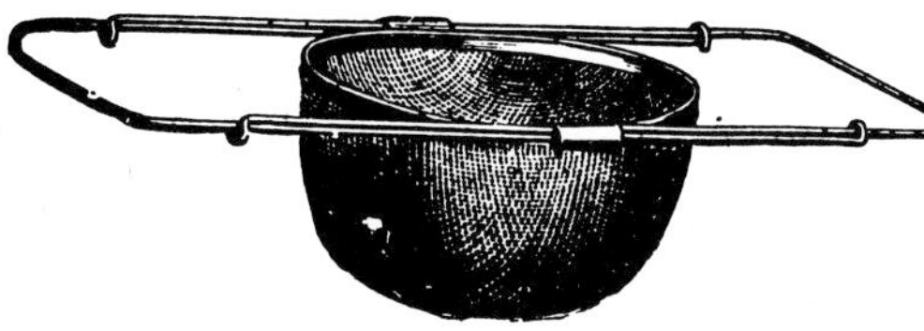

The Housekeeper Cook Book *was published by Buckeye Cook Books of Minneapolis in 1894. This copy belonged to Mary A. Buklin who signed the flyleaf and added notes for a "Sure Cure for Cancer." Courtesy, Olmsted County Historical Society*

told to soften water with ashes, sort fine cloth from coarse, scald table linens, scrub laundry in hot water, blue laundry in cool water, wring out the wash, starch selected items, hang the laundry out to dry, shake to remove wrinkles, iron clothes, and finally fold the laundry. One wonders if housewives had the energy to put clean clothes away.

Prospectors were doing a vastly different kind of work during the 1860s. Using gold rockers (devices to separate gold from sand), they eagerly sifted through black sand found in a drift along the Zumbro River. Astonishingly, they found gold fragments in Lower Magnesian strata. The result was Rochester's three-day gold rush. Prospectors raced each other to set up gold rockers along streambeds from Rochester to Oronoco. More gold was found!

Aleck Fleck had visions of becoming a millionaire until his pals admitted they had salted his gold rocker with a handful of brass filings. Lucius Renslow had slightly better luck. He found enough gold to fill a glass medicine vial halfway. But the cash value of his find did not even cover his prospecting expenses. Other prospectors had similar results and Rochester's gold rush fizzled as abruptly as it had started.

Daily chores did not leave people with much leisure time. When they had time, Rochester residents eagerly read newspapers such as the *Rochester Democrat,* which began publication in 1857. The *Rochester Democrat,* which had an eight-column format, failed after only two years of publication. In 1858 the *Rochester Free Press* began publication, followed the next year by the *Rochester City News.*

Also in 1859 the *Rochester City Post* was founded and became known as a Republican paper. "As the majority of the people in the county were of the same political stripe, it could hardly fail of success," commented historian W.H. Mitchell. The *Rochester Daily Bulletin* began publication in 1891. On May 30, 1925, these two newspapers were consolidated into the *Rochester Post-Bulletin.*

thing on the prairie that swam, walked, grew, or flew. Directions for broiled pheasant (prairie chicken could be substituted) are amusing today. Readers were told to scald, skin, de-shot, boil, *and* broil the bird, which could be eaten immediately or served for breakfast on top of fried mush.

Today just reading the laundry chapter is tiring enough. Housewives were

Foreign-language newspapers ap
peared early in Rochester but many
were short-lived. The *Nordisk Fokeblad,*
founded in 1868, managed to garner statewide readership. Edited by Sundorf Christian, a Danish emigrant, the paper was a subsidiary of the earlier *Rochester Post* (the
word "City" was dropped from its name
in 1865). Within the first nine months of publication, the paper had a circulation of
3,000 readers throughout Minnesota.

From the turbulence of early days,
law and order gradually emerged. Rochester, which had been in competition with
Oronoco, was selected as the seat of Olmsted County in 1857. One year later
Moses Fay was elected mayor, assisted
by a city justice, treasurer, recorder, mar-
shal, and editor of the city's official newspaper, the *Rochester Free Press.* By April
1858 the population of Rochester had
soared to 106 people. Population continued to climb, and in March 1869 the city
was divided into five districts.

Clearly, Rochester needed a courthouse. Until one could be designed and
built, the city rented the Broadway
House, which locals considered the city's
finest hotel. Rochester made maximum
use of the three-story building, using the
first floor as a schoolhouse, the second
floor as a courthouse, and the top floor
as a meeting hall. Meanwhile, a committee was organized to investigate land purchase and courthouse design.

In 1865 three acres of land were purchased for the future site of the courthouse at a cost of $800. Committee
members stipulated that the courthouse
must be built of brick, stone, or a combination of both materials, and be constructed at a minimum cost of $15,000.
By 1866 the courthouse was almost complete and legal records were transferred
from the Broadway House into the new
building. According to Burt W. Eaton, a
Rochester lawyer, the $32,000 courthouse
was financed by collection of delinquent

Built in 1862, the Dee log cabin was one of Rochester's oldest dwellings. Burt Eaton, a Rochester lawyer, said the cabin was built by 25 work-men in one day. The cabin was built with poplar logs, bought at a cost of approxi-mately $25. William Dee, a shoemaker, his wife, and their four children lived in the cabin for 15 years. Cour-tesy, Olmsted County Histori-cal Society

taxes, accrued interest, and treasury funds.

A variety of ordinances were passed concerning issues such as "houses of ill repute," feeding prisoners bread and water, stray swine running loose, and public bathing in streams. One ordinance prohibited fast driving on bridges, a necessity to prevent collapse due to weight or vibration. The ordinance was explicit: "Whoever shall drive any horse, mule, ox or cow upon or over any bridge in the city of Rochester faster than a walk, or who shall drive upon or over such bridge more than fifteen head of horses or cattle at a time, shall be deemed guilty of a misdemeanor . . ." This offense was punishable by fine and/or imprisonment.

Government services expanded to meet the demands of a burgeoning population. In 1855 Rochester's first post office opened in a log cabin near Cascade Creek. During the first quarter of business, Postmaster Robert McReady took in gross receipts of $13.06. Postal rates were based upon mileage: five cents for each letter mailed a distance less than 300 miles. Mail was transported by the Walker Stage Line along the Dubuque Trail.

Stagecoaches were actually open wagons without handrails. The rattling coaches left St. Paul three times a week and took four to five days to make the 272-mile journey to Dubuque. Travel time depended upon weather conditions. Rochester had several access routes to the Dubuque Trail in case one route was mired in mud or closed by snow. Passengers were allowed to ride along but did so at their own peril.

Mrs. Joseph Ullman chronicled her trip to Dubuque in a manuscript, "Saint Paul Forty Years Ago." She and her husband rode the entire length of the trail from St. Paul to Dubuque in "a wooden bed crossed by board seats." The sledge, as Mrs. Ullman called it, was filled with straw. Each passenger was provided with a rake to distribute the straw. Two horses pulled the stagecoach, which left on time as stipulated by contract. When blizzards made the trail invisible, the stagecoach driver had to rely on the horses to find the way.

Stagecoaches stopped at small log huts where passengers could buy food and occasionally spirits, and sleep in a common room partitioned—if they were lucky by blankets. Supper, which cost from $1 to $1.50, was invariably the same— bacon and potatoes. According to Mrs. Ullman she was given "a cloth stiff from grease and dirt, a fork with broken prongs, a knife with a greasy wooden handle was the spread; a dish of greasy looking liquid in which floated one piece of fat pork, boiled potatoes with the dirt remaining on them, and a piece of sad, heavy hot bread . . ."

The Rochester Fire Department purchased a fire engine in July 1870. Nicknamed Little Giant, the engine cost $9,500. Three months later an engine house was completed and fire department officers—chief, chief engineer, secretary, treasurer, and foreman—were elected. The department was divided into companies, one company for each horse carriage. Each company had its own name, some rather glamorous such as "The Night Hawk Hose Company."

As with any new venture it took time

Facing page, top: During 1902 the Rochester Fire Board ordered that fire escapes be installed in three city buildings. Chief Boylhart had new swinging hose racks installed in the firehouse; each rack held 100 feet of hose. The firemen were called for duty 32 times; new uniforms were purchased for all the firemen; and the year ended with a traditional fireman's ball. Courtesy, Olmsted County Historical Society

Facing page, bottom: Lyman Tondro (seated at left with cane), one of Rochester's first millers, owned the Cascade Mills. He served as postmaster, assisted by his daughter, Mrs. Florence Tondro Goodrich, who served as clerk. All four Rochester mail carriers are standing in the back row. Courtesy, Olmsted County Historical Society

Left: The handsome, ornate, Central Station firehouse was located at the end of Broadway. Courtesy, Olmsted County Historical Society

for the fire department to achieve cohesion. "The organization of the fire department was delayed by difficulties usually encountered by public enterprises until December, 1870," commented W.H. Hill in *History of Olmsted County, Minnesota.* Eventually two massive cisterns were constructed to support fire department efforts.

One oval cistern was built at the corner of Fourth and Main. Little Giant's steam engine filled the 700-barrel cisterns with river water, pumping at a rate of one inch per minute. Rochester was proud of these construction projects, especially the quality of materials and workmanship. The *Rochester Post* reported on July 1, 1871, "They are both built by Mr. Thomas Ireland, well known as a first class workman."

With the construction of a pumping station on Fourth Street in 1887 and the construction of a sheriff's office and jail in 1888, Rochester had an array of city services. Members of the five-man police force worked 12-hour shifts. Their primary responsibility was rounding up vagrants and drunks. Ludwig Ranfranz, in his first year on the force, picked up 15 vagrants and 2 drunks. But the number of vagrants continued to increase, and in 1897 a total of 105 was picked up. Most vagrants were picked up in an area near the Chicago & North Western Railroad tracks, where they congregated.

As the city grew, Broadway became a wide thoroughfare lined with wooden storefronts. Hitching posts stood like sentinels along both sides of the street. Horse-drawn buggies were tied to the posts, often jammed wheel-to-wheel. That the

city had prospered is clear. Three factors contributed to Rochester's rapid growth, indeed, to its very survival: its midcontinent location, the Dubuque Trail, and the coming of the railroad.

Rochester's location, an accident of history, proved critical to its development. As Thomas F. Waters observed in his book *The Streams and Rivers of Minnesota,* the state "lies astride the transition between eastern woodlands and the Western prairies, from northern coniferous forests to the corn belt of mid-nation . . ." The settlement's location provided pioneers with drinking water, natural drainage, mill power, and transportation. Later this location served as a junction point for westward expansion.

Towns literally sprang up overnight along the Dubuque Trail. Dusty, winding, and at times frightening, this rough track linked the prairie towns together. After the Mississippi River had frozen solid and steamboat traffic ceased, the Dubuque Trail was the only link between towns. Landseekers, many escaping the drudgery of the smoking, eastern factories, followed the trail to Rochester. Essentially, the village became one vast community campground. Cooking fires flickered brightly and covered wagons (called prairie schooners) rimmed the encampment. Many pioneers, who appreciated the beauty of the heartland and saw its potential, decided to remain here.

Travel along the Dubuque Trail reached its peak around 1861. By this time stagecoaches had been vastly improved, sporting plush seats, windows, and water-repellent roofs. With the arrival of the railroads, stagecoach travel along the Dubuque Trail dwindled. The Winona and St. Peter Railroad (which later became the Chicago & North Western) was the first to initiate service, its wood-burning engine puffing into Rochester during the summer of 1864.

Marion Sloan, a 15-year-old teacher, recorded the historic event in her diary. Her terse entries convey the excitement of the time:

October 8th, 1864—A passenger car came in today for the FIRST TIME.

October 9th, 1864—We walked down to look at the engines, "Winona" and "Rochester." They are beautiful specimens of art.

October 10, 1864—I saw the passenger cars come in and the people come out of the cars. One very old lady and a poor sick soldier came.

Next to begin service was the Winona and Southwestern Railroad, with tracks that ran from Winona through High Forest Township. Stagecoaches met the trains and transported passengers to Owatonna, Mankato, St. Peter, and other southeastern towns. In 1903 the Great Western Railroad Company began service to Rochester. However, not everyone greeted railroad service with the enthusiasm of the young Marion Sloan.

One of the city's first settlers, Thomas Cummings, was dead set against the railroad because the tracks would slice across his northwest Rochester land. When the grading crew showed up for work, the tight-lipped Cummings became so irate that the frightened foreman shot him in the chest. An agitated crowd gathered and, fearing a lynching, several residents hustled the foreman out of town. Fortunately, Cummings survived the near-fatal attack.

After years of bickering, false starts, and failed bond issues, railroad service expanded. The Chicago & North Western Railroad received a $30,000 bond bonus from Rochester, as well as bonuses from

The Plummer Building was named in honor of Dr. Henry Plummer, who supervised its construction. A green and white flashing beacon atop the tower guided aircraft into Rochester. Courtesy, Mayo Clinic

Zumbrota and Pine Island. "Transients could reach Rochester by train, and the Chicago & North Western tapped the large eastern populous sections and extended on into the growing Dakotas, which attracted large numbers of settlers in the eighties," wrote a newspaperman. City incentives and approval of spur lines did much to stimulate railroad expansion.

Spur lines enabled farmers to sell their grain locally. The Winona and St. Peter Railroad, for example, ran a spur line to the Zumbro Flouring Mill. Ordinance 32, published in 1881, stipulated that the Winona and St. Peter would construct, operate, and maintain the railroad track which ran slightly beyond the mill. Additional grain elevators were built beside the tracks, where railroad cars were efficiently loaded. Wheat was shipped to central midwestern markets such as Milwaukee and Chicago.

Looking like a miniature village beside a toy train track, Rochester snuggled amidst the farmlands of southeastern Minnesota—a pastoral scene. The economic base of the community was agriculture, and probably would have remained so, but a small incident drastically altered the course of history. Dr. William Worrall Mayo moved to town.

Early participating partners of the Mayo Clinic turned out to welcome Sir Rickman Goldee, president of the Royal College of Surgeons. From left to right are: Dr. E. Starr Judd, Dr. Will, Sir Goldee, Dr. Christopher Graham, Dr. Charlie, and Dr. Donald C. Balfour. Courtesy, Mayo Clinic

2

THREE DOCTORS NAMED MAYO

It was mid-May of 1863 when Dr. William Worrall Mayo, under the Enrollment Act, assumed his duties as a Civil War examining surgeon. Dr. Mayo had left his family behind in Le Sueur and arrived in Rochester alone.

From its inception in 1861 to its cessation in 1865, the Civil War had a profound effect upon Rochester families. The population of Olmsted County was roughly 12,000, and 1,250 males went off to fight. Records filed in the Minnesota State Adjutant's office showed 250 casualties from Rochester, one Rochester soldier for every five Minnesota soldiers killed.

Minnesota in the Civil and Indian Wars, Volume I, published under the auspice of a state commission, listed the name of every soldier who served in the war. Comments beside the names, such as musician, died of smallpox, resigned, and deserted give us a keyhole glimpse of history. The phrase "killed at Gettysburg" appears repeatedly like a mournful refrain.

Recruits of the Minnesota First Regiment, whose members came from the entire southern half of the state, were poorly equipped at the start of the war. The regiment's commander wrote to Governor Alexander Ramsey, Commander-in-Chief, requesting uniforms for the 867 recruits as well as shoes, flannel shirts, caps, 1,734 pairs of socks, knapsacks, canteens, tents, cooking utensils, axes, and picks or spades.

In addition to giving soldiers their induction physicals, Dr. Mayo had to be on the alert for draft dodgers and aware of the winds of public opinion. His position as Civil War examining surgeon was not a respected one. Public sentiment was against the war, and draftees could hire replacements, an act viewed by some as cowardly. Despite these difficulties Dr. Mayo liked the town and decided to settle in Rochester. He purchased two adjoining lots, contracted for a house, and moved his family from Le Sueur to Rochester in 1864.

Dr. Mayo had married Louise Wright in 1851 (taking close friends by surprise) and they had six children. Their first-born, a son, died when he was six weeks old. Gertrude was born in 1853 and Phoebe in 1859. Another daughter, Sarah, died when she was a just over one year old. William was born in 1861, followed by Charles in 1865.

The Mayo boys, as they came to be called, learned medicine from their father. They accompanied him on rounds, carried medical supplies, prepared microscopic slides, and, as they grew older, assisted with autopsies. In *The Doctors Mayo* Helen Clapesattle includes an excerpt by Will describing how he was left alone in the Bradley House hotel to complete a postmortem: "I can feel it yet," Will wrote many years later, "the weird atmosphere of that squeaky old house with its long shadowy corridors, and I remember that struggle I had to complete the job and force myself to walk slowly out the front door."

Some think Louise Mayo deserved equal credit for Will and Charlie becoming physicians. An intellectual in her own right, she pursued interests in astronomy and botany, assisted her husband with surgery, applied splints, and listened to patients' complaints when Dr. W.W. was out on a call. She even cooked meals for waiting patients. Her medical education was gleaned from on-the-job training and persistent study of her husband's textbooks. "Mother was a real good doctor herself," commented Charlie.

Louise Mayo was a woman of insight. Writing to her friend Carrie France, she chided herself about misspelled words that were "too much work to hunt up in the dictionary." She advised her friend to take an interest in people, "not caring for the high minded or intellectual—but the poor who have a care for material things—struggling for a chance to live, to grow . . ."

Louise also gave her husband the chance to grow. When Dr. W.W. traveled the world ("a veritable vagabond," according to Clapesattle), it was Louise who kept the household running. When family finances grew short, it was Louise who supplemented the family income by working as a milliner. When her husband wanted a modern microscope, it was Louise who grudgingly approved mortgaging their house to finance the purchase. Of her life in southeastern Minnesota, Louise commented, "It was a hard country."

Will and Charlie were close brothers, yet quite different in personality. Charlie loved working on the family farm, chopping wood, hauling water, and herding cows, but Will hated farm work and much preferred working at Geisinger and Newton's drug store. The family decided the boys would benefit from attending different medical schools, so Will took his three years of training at the University of Michigan and Charlie attended Northwestern University. After graduation the young physicians returned home to help their father.

These were the days of kitchen surgery, when operations were performed on tables, spare couches, or a door suspended between two sawhorses. As a logical outgrowth of his medical prac-

This Civil War belt buckle belonged to Milo Crumb, a local soldier from the High Forest Township. Milo Crumb was shot on January 17, 1862, and died three days later. His family donated the belt buckle to the Olmsted County Historical Society. Courtesy, Olmsted County Historical Society

Four generations of Mayos are represented in this portrait. Seated on the left is Louise Mayo, wife of Dr. W.W. On the right is her daughter, Gertrude Berkman. Standing is Gertrude's daughter, Martha Blethen, wife of attorney Ralph Blethen, and Martha's daughter, Joan, sits between her grandmother and great-grandmother. Courtesy, Olmsted County Historical Society

tice, Dr. W.W. became a partner in O.W. Anderson's drugstore. A notice in the *Rochester Post* on November 30, 1867, reported, "He [Anderson] has entered into a partnership with Dr. Mayo who will be associated with him in the drug business hereafter. It would be difficult to get up a better firm, than so excellent a druggist as Anderson and so excellent a physician as Mayo."

Dr. W.W. began sending his sons out on medical calls, and slowly but surely Will and Charlie earned reputations as respectable physicians. The Doctors Mayo knew about the work of the Sisters of Saint Francis in Rochester, a local teaching order supervised by Mother Alfred. "It was a tornado, however, that literally blew the Sisters of St. Francis and the Doctors Mayo together," explained Barbara Callahan in her article, "The Doctors Mayo and the Sisters."

On August 21, 1883, residents anxiously watched the sky as dark, swirling cloud formations hovered over the city. Suddenly, the clouds merged, rain began to fall, and a roaring tornado touched down. (The first written accounts referred to the storm as a "cyclone.") An area called Lower Town felt the full brunt of the storm. Houses were blown off their foundations. Trees were eerily stripped bare of leaves. Blades of grass pierced some tree trunks like needles. Dead livestock littered the countryside. When the Whiting family emerged from their basement, they found themselves looking at open sky. Their house had been unroofed though the table was still neatly set for supper!

Telegraph lines had snapped during the tornado. Someone jury-rigged a line into the main line, and on this feeble connection a message was tapped to Governor Lucius F. Hubbard. The code was chillingly brief: "Rochester is in ruins. Twenty-four people were killed. Over forty are seriously injured. One-third of

the city laid waste. We need immediate help. S. Whitten, Mayor."

By some quirk of fate, leading businessmen were meeting with the governor when the message was received in St. Paul. Within 40 minutes Governor Hubbard raised $5,000 in relief funds. Minneapolis pledged $5,000, St. Paul pledged $5,000, and Chicago pledged an additional $10,000. Other communities donated funds, pushing the total to $60,441.51. Mayor Samuel Whitten appointed a disaster relief committee. Interestingly, no Mayo names were on it, but this was inconsequential since the three Mayo doctors were already hard at work.

While Dr. Will and Dr. Charlie treated patients at the Mayos' office, Dr. W.W. was treating patients at the Buck Hotel. The "old doctor" had a difference of opinion with another physician who wanted to administer emetics to the injured—a common practice. Dr. Mayo argued that patients who just survived a tornado did not need the added indignity of vomiting. His opinion prevailed, and Dr. Mayo was appointed chairman of relief efforts

by the city council. He turned to the Sisters of Saint Francis for help.

Months later, echoing the suggestion of the Reverend John Ireland, Bishop of St. Paul, Mother Alfred proposed construction of a hospital to be staffed by the Doctors Mayo. Nursing care would be provided by the Sisters of Saint Francis. Dr. W.W. quickly discounted the idea, saying Rochester was too small to support a hospital and construction costs would be prohibitive. Mother Alfred modified her proposal. If the Sisters raised construction funds, would he then agree? His answer was yes.

The Sisters of Saint Francis raised $40,000 by living at a subsistence level, selling needlework projects, giving music lessons, and taking odd jobs. Controversy ensued. Worried residents wondered if St. Marys (the proposed hospital) would admit non-Catholic patients. Mother Alfred tried to calm their concern, replying that illness was a medical, not a religious, condition. Accordingly, St. Marys would treat patients of all races and religions. Furthermore, paying and nonpaying patients would receive equal treatment.

Mother Alfred's dream became a reality when the 27-bed hospital opened in 1889. St. Marys was state-of-the-art for its time, equipped with an operating room lit by natural light, water spigots in hallways in case of fire, and a special ventilating system to dispel noxious odors. Several months later a bell system was installed so patients could summon nurses. Before the hospital was officially opened, Dr. Will and Dr. Charlie performed surgery for eye cancer, assisted by their father, who served as the anesthetist.

No exact date can be cited for the founding of Mayo Clinic. Rather, Mayo Clinic evolved from the working relationship between the Sisters of Saint Francis and the Doctors Mayo. *Sketch of the History of the Mayo Clinic and Mayo Foundation* reported:

As the practice grew and developed, it attracted the attention of other physicians and surgeons who came for the purposes of observation and study; these visitors came in increasing numbers and gradually came to speak of the work as the "Mayo Clinic" until it eventually came to be referred to and called by that name, not only in the profession but by laity . . .

By 1893 St. Marys had provided medical care for over 1,000 patients—an incredible number for such a small hospital. Three factors contributed to St. Marys' success: the Sisters of Saint Francis, sterile techniques, and centralization of the Mayos' medical practice.

The selfless caring of the Sisters of Saint Francis, whose workday began around 3 A.M., is almost beyond belief. They walked into Rochester to buy groceries, cooked meals for the patients, carried trays up and down stairs, washed and ironed all the hospital linens, pumped water from the 500-gallon basement cistern, shoveled coal into the fiery furnace, and kept continuous watch to prevent patients from falling down empty elevator shafts. When the sewage system backed up, the sisters took care of that, too. In 1898, at the sisters' expense, St. Marys

was connected with the city sewage system.

Mother Alfred was a woman of steely determination. Born on November 1, 1829, in Reimich, Luxembourg, she was educated in France and immigrated to the United States in the 1850s. Eventually she made her way to Rochester where she supervised the construction of a convent. Twenty-five sisters originally lived in the convent, but as their numbers increased the sisters opened schools in five other midwestern states.

Sadly though, after St. Marys opened, Mother Alfred was unable to savor the fruits of her labors. Influenced by complaints from sisters who thought nursing was a lesser calling, Archbishop John Ireland transferred Mother Alfred from St. Marys. She was returned to her educational mission in St. Paul and served in this capacity until her death on December 18, 1899. Two days after her death the *Olmsted County Democrat* hailed the establishment of St. Marys Hospital

Mother Alfred wanted St. Marys Hospital to feel as homey as possible. Rooms were furnished with wicker chairs, tables, and screens. Brightly colored bedspreads decorated the iron beds. Although gaslight fixtures were installed in each room, there was no fuel for the lights. Thus, it was necessary for the Sisters of Saint Francis to carry lanterns as they made their rounds. Courtesy, Olmsted County Historical Society

as Mother Alfred's crowning achievement.

The Mayos thought they could accomplish more by teamwork. And work they did. "Until 1893 the Doctors Mayo, themselves, attended to all the work at the hospital and clinic. They operated at St. Mary's from 8 A.M. until 1 or 2 P.M., then attended to the work at the clinic and in the evening visited the patients at St. Mary's. When a physician was needed at the hospital during the night, they answered the call," reported *A Souvenir of St. Mary's Hospital.*

Hospital records for 1893 list 405 operations performed by the Doctors Mayo. Realizing they needed help, they hired Dr. Augustus Stinchfield, an Eyota physician, as their first partner in 1892, followed by Dr. Christopher Graham in 1894. Mayo Clinic expanded at a steady rate and by 1914 there were 17 perma-

nent physicians on its staff. During its first 32 years St. Marys Hospital treated 112,817 patients—an impressive statistic considering that the public at the turn of the century viewed hospitals as asylums, places to vegetate or die.

Under the Mayos, who had studied the work of Dr. Joseph Lister and applied his sterile technique, public perceptions changed. The Doctors Mayo were among the first physicians to wear rubber gloves (invented by Dr. William Halsted in 1890) and to use a portable sterilizer. Mortality figures dropped markedly. In four and a half years at St. Marys, Dr. Will and Dr. Charlie jointly performed 655 operations. Their success rate was a stunning 98.3 percent.

For 10 years the brothers operated together. "As the number of operations mounted, it became an impractical expenditure of time and ability for Dr. Will and

Dr. Charlie to serve as each other's assistant. So they combined their efforts in fewer and fewer instances until finally the separation of their operating schedules was virtually complete," reported Helen Clapesattle. Dr. Will specialized in pelvic and abdominal surgery; Dr. Charlie in diseases of the eye, ear, nose, throat, and neck.

By the early 1900s Dr. W.W. was no longer practicing medicine but concentrating on travel, politics, and research. While studying how to extract alcohol from decaying plants and animal wastes, Dr. W.W. crushed his hand and forearm in a machine. Three successive operations did not correct the injury and, as a last resort, his hand and lower forearm were amputated. Age and poor health took their toll. On March 6, 1911, a few months before his 92nd birthday, Dr. William Worrall Mayo died. In tribute the Rochester schools closed, flags were flown at half-mast, and businesses closed their doors during the funeral service.

Dr. Will and Dr. Charlie continued the work their father had started. Because hospital space was a major problem, five additions were added to St. Marys Hospital: one in 1893, one in 1898, one in 1904, one in 1908, and the last in 1912. About the time the first addition was built, the American Protective Association conducted a propaganda campaign against St. Marys. Some Protestant ministers joined the campaign and, together, these groups managed to raise sufficient funds to build a competitive facility called Riverside Hospital.

The Doctors Mayo refused to operate at Riverside Hospital and steadfastly continued their work at St. Marys. At Riverside, "a famous homeopathic surgeon was very unsuccessful and, the confidence of the community being shaken, patients were not forthcoming," reported *Sketch of the History of Mayo Clinic and the Mayo Foundation.* Not surprisingly, Riverside Hospital failed.

Up to their rubber gloves in surgery, the Doctors Mayo had little time to devote to the business side of their prac-

tice. In 1908 they hired Harry Harwick away from the First National Bank, where he had been employed as a teller. Dr. Will personally interviewed Harwick, explained that the firm needed someone to initiate accounting and business systems, and offered him a salary of $75 a month.

With only a diploma from Winona High School, Harwick felt apprehensive about working at Mayo Clinic. Nonetheless, he accepted the challenge. "I liked this town, wanted to stay and grow with it. I knew that this was a wonderful opportunity—if I could measure up to it," explained Harwick in *Forty-Four Years with the Mayo Clinic.* On his 21st birthday Harwick went from shoveling walks and shuffling papers to streamlining the Mayo ledger-card system and implementing new purchase systems.

A friend of both Dr. Will and Dr. Charlie, Harwick thought the brothers had complementary personalities. He characterized Dr. Will as a natural leader, reserved, analytical, and dominating—in a kindly sort of way—with high ideals for himself and others. Dr. Charlie was described as gregarious, understanding, and humorous, a man who possessed the common touch. "The first and perhaps greatest lesson I learned from the Mayos was that of teamwork," wrote Harwick. "For 'my brother and I' was no mere convenient term of reference, but rather an expression of basic, indivisible philosophy of life."

As the waiting list grew progressively longer, St. Marys Hospital expansion projects failed to keep pace with the increasing patient load. In an attempt to alleviate the problem, John Kahler remodeled the former Knowlton mansion into a hospital-hotel, where patients stayed before and after surgery. This care unit grew into the Kahler Corporation. Other hotels and hospitals were erected, including the 235-bed Colonial Hospital. Orthopedic, urologic, and general surgeries were performed at the Colonial, which also handled emergencies.

The Mayos also practiced at the Rochester State Hospital, previously called Sec-

Mayowood was the country home of Dr. and Mrs. Charles H. Mayo. The 3,000-acre estate was located outside of Rochester on wooded land adjoining the Zumbro River. Numerous antiques furnished the 38-room villa. From the Aeolian organ in the music room to the rocking horse in the nursery, Mayowood reflected the generations of Mayos who lived there. In 1965 the villa and 10 acres of surrounding land were donated to the Olmsted County Historical Society. Courtesy, Mayo Clinic

ond State Hospital for the Insane. Opened in 1879, the facility was unique in that it was totally self-sufficient, a city within a city. Rochester State Hospital had an independent water supply, operating dairy, railroad spur line, tailor shop, laundry, dry cleaning plant, harness shop (which also did shoe repair), upholstery shop, cannery, slaughterhouse, smokehouse, and brick kiln.

The Worrall Hospital opened in 1919, specializing in eye, ear, nose, and throat care; dental surgery; neurology; dermatology; and syphilology. In 1920 the Curie Hospital opened, specializing in diseases treated by radiation. Still another hospi-

tal, the Samaritan, owned by the Evangelical Church of Peace, opened in 1922. Contagious cases were handled by St. Marys Isolation Hospital, a separate unit opened in 1918.

John Kahler opened the 60-room Kahler Hotel in 1907, an updated version of the hospital-hotel concept. The top five floors of the hotel were designated as medical floors, with surgery and obstetrics on the topmost floor. Decades later, because of mounting costs, changing legislation, and tax structures, the Kahler Corporation found it could not continue to operate hotels and hospitals.

The administration sought help from Harry Harwick (then Kahler's secretary-treasurer), who in turn sought the help of Slade Schuster, Ralph Jester, Roy Watson, Sr., Roy Watson, Jr., and Harry Blackmun, now associate justice of the Supreme Court. Blackmun wrote to the officials of the Minnesota Conference of Methodist Churches, based in Minneapolis. After long-term study the Methodist church bought the hospitals, continuing affiliation with Mayo Clinic. Without interrupting patient care Worrall Hospital and Kahler Hospital were incorporated as Rochester Methodist Hospital on January 1, 1954.

As their wealth accumulated, Dr. Will and Dr. Charlie generously supported the beautification and development of Rochester. They donated funds to the Rochester Board of Education to hire a band director. They gave the city two blocks of land, which became St. Marys Park, and 40 acres of land west of the Zumbro River, which became Mayo Park. Dr. Will and Dr. Charlie established the Mayo Foundation for Medical Education and Research, endowing the University of Minnesota with $1,650,344.79.

This endowment to the university, however, had raised a bitter public dispute which seemed to be based on the politics of envy. The motives of Dr. Will and Dr. Charlie were questioned. Was the proposed endowment really a slick publicity gimmick? Debate continued for months until, on September 17, 1917, Mayo Clinic affiliated with the University of Minnesota. Dr. Will explained his philosophy in a letter to the university:

Our father recognized certain definite social obligations. He believed that any man who had better opportunity than others, greater strength of mind, body, or character, owed something to those who had not been so provided; that is, that the important thing in life is not to accomplish for one's self alone, but for each to carry his share of collective responsibility.

According to the original agreement, income from the endowment fund was added to the principal, which made the Mayos' donation to the University of Minnesota an even $2 million.

As Dr. Will and Dr. Charlie approached middle age, they made plans to safeguard the future of Mayo Clinic. Thus, the Mayo Properties Association was established to finance medical education and research. A committee was appointed to study the problem, composed of Harry Harwick, Judge George Granger, and Burt W. Eaton. Lawyers, judges, University of Minnesota officials, and a Winona attorney, Leslie L. Brown, were consulted.

Dr. Will had two daughters, Carrie, born in 1887, and Phoebe, born in 1897. Carrie married Dr. Donald Balfour. Phoebe married Dr. Waltman Walters. Phoebe described her father as a great surgeon, natural leader, extremely modest man, and "my best friend." Courtesy, Mayo Clinic

For more than a year Harwick, Judge Granger, and Eaton commuted to Winona to meet with Brown and his law partner. Together these men hammered out the terms of the legal agreement which established the association. On October 8, 1919, Dr. Will and Dr. Charlie signed the agreement, which stipulated that all present and future earnings were to be turned over to a charitable corporation. And the profits accumulated by the corporation would be "judiciously expended to promote medical education and research." Harwick, Judge Granger, Eaton, and others became trustees of $10.5 million. This nonprofit corporation evolved into the present-day Mayo Foundation.

Surely these fiscal decisions shaped the future of Mayo Clinic, as did the work of Dr. Henry Plummer. Dr. Will considered Dr. Plummer the "best brain the Clinic ever had." In an article entitled "The Work of Dr. Henry S. Plummer," Dr. Will wrote, "Developing many things along many diverse lines, always he came back to his fundamental work on the thyroid gland, in which he was no less than a genius." Dr. Plummer's genius reached far beyond his specialty of bronchoscopy.

Dr. Plummer designed the patient history record form, enabling Mayo Clinic to track records independently; the cross-index system, based upon a coding system of envelopes still used today; and unique surgical instruments, which he crafted in his home workshop. The intra-clinic phone system was also the brainstorm of Dr. Plummer, as was the compressed-air system that shoots records between Mayo Clinic and St. Marys, and a system of underground walkways called the subway. "Henry's mind was never satisfied," added Dr. Will.

Because of his intense power of concentration, which Dr. Will called "a scientific trance," Henry Plummer became known as an eccentric genius. He ate the same lunch every day in the same restaurant. Sometimes Dr. Plummer forgot he had eaten and ordered lunch again. His wife, Daisy, a cousin of Phoebe Mayo Walters, cheerfully accepted her husband's absent-mindedness. Away for a visit she wrote him, "Don't forget to water the pots in the kitchen windows and be sure to put in the sweet peas."

Dr. Plummer closely supervised every aspect of the Plummer Building's construction, from the handsome stone reliefs which adorn the exterior to the marble walls and floors and lavishly decorated ceilings inside. Elevators in the Plummer Building had to accommodate traffic surges, so Dr. Plummer met with the Otis chief engineer to discuss the problem. Afterward, the engineer remarked that Dr. Plummer knew far more about elevators than he did.

On December 31, 1936, Dr. Plummer left work and headed for home. On the way he began to feel ill and diagnosed his illness as bulbar paralysis, a stroke in the bulbar area of the brain. Dr. Plummer pulled into the garage and from there was assisted into the house, where he summoned family members to tell them that within the hour he would be unconscious. "As long as that intelligence which had carried him through life was permitted to function, he traced the progress of his last illness," recalled Dr. Will. Dr. Henry Plummer died just as he had predicted, and the massive bronze doors of the building named in his honor were closed in silent tribute.

Like their father and Dr. Plummer, the Mayo brothers contributed to the growth and prosperity of Rochester. True hometown boys, both brothers married local girls. Hattie Damon became Will's bride in November 1884. Despite growing fame and financial security, Dr. Will and Hattie endured their share of tragedy. Three of their five children died in infancy, survived by Carrie and Phoebe. Charles married Edith Graham, his father's personally trained anesthetist. The newlyweds moved into a red frame house on College Street. Two of their eight children died in infancy. Close as boys, Dr. Will and Dr. Charlie became even closer as men, trusting each other to such an extent that they shared a common bank account.

Dr. Charlie settled his family into a 40-room villa on 3,000 acres of rolling woodland outside Rochester. Built of stone, reinforced concrete, and tile, the sprawling mansion was completed in 1911. Legend says Dr. Charlie mapped out the home during a family picnic by laying string on the ground. Visitors including Helen Keller, Franklin Roosevelt, Adlai Stevenson, the king of Nepal, and King Faisal of Saudi Arabia signed the Mayos' guest book. "The gracious lady of the household and her distinguished husband radiate happiness and good will to the many who enjoy their hospitality," noted *Sketch of the History of the Mayo Clinic and the Mayo Foundation.*

Dr. Will settled his family in a three-story Tudor mansion (four stories if you count the tower) close to the heart of the city. The 45-room home was made of cut stone and was surrounded by lush, informal gardens which dropped down the hillside. A large portico, overlooking a semi-circular brick drive, graced the front of the home. When his daughter Phoebe married Dr. Waltman Walters in 1921, Dr. Will built a house for them on the oppo-

On August 8, 1934, President Franklin D. Roosevelt came to Rochester to present Dr. Will and Dr. Charlie with National American Legion citations. The ceremony was held at Soldiers Field. An estimated 125,000 people witnessed the awarding of the plaques. President Roosevelt's remarks and the Mayo acceptance remarks were broadcast over two nationwide radio networks. Courtesy, Olmsted County Historical Society

33

site corner of the block. Recalled Phoebe, "Father had a red brick walk laid from their house to ours, which, he joked, was Mother's Christmas and birthday gift for that year. Every year after that, if he forgot her birthday (and was gently reminded of it by others), he would point out that her gift was 'the red brick walk.'"

The Mayo brothers died within two months of each other. Dr. Charlie died in Chicago on May 26, 1939, after an eight-day bout with pneumonia. Dr. Will died on July 28, 1939, from complications following surgery for stomach cancer. Again the solid bronze doors of the Plummer Building, standing 16 feet high and weighing 4,000 pounds each, were closed in tribute. An era had ended.

City growth paralleled the growth of Mayo Clinic. The Rochester Board of Trade was established in 1884 and publicized the diversity of city businesses, including a furniture factory, boiler factory, venetian blind factory, seed separator factory, foundries, and an anvil and vise works. Along Broadway, banners, flags, and billboards advertised shopowners' wares. R.L. Tollefson & Company invested in upscale advertising for the time—sachet envelopes with a poem printed on them. Entitled "Reciprocity," the poem read:

*The young lady is very affectionate—and
THAT'S HER BUSINESS!
The young man appreciates her affection—
THAT'S HIS BUSINESS!
Their affections grow to love and they marry—
THAT'S THEIR BUSINESS!
Then when they need anything in the line of furniture, carpets, rugs, linoleums, curtains, shades, and draperies,
THAT'S OUR BUSINESS!*

In 1950 Dr. Edward C. Kendall (seated) and Dr. Philip S. Hench (standing) received the Nobel Prize in Medicine for their work in the development of Cortisone. The two Mayo Clinic physicians shared the prize with a Swiss physician, Dr. Tadeusz Richstein. Courtesy, Mayo Clinic

OUTSTANDING MAYO CLINIC ACCOMPLISHMENTS

1905   Dr. Louis Wilson develops frozen tissue technique.

1922   Mayo physicians are first to use iodine to successfully treat goiters.

1933   First blood bank is established.

1942   One of the earliest human centrifuges ever built is installed in the Medical Sciences Building. Experiments using the centrifuge lead to the development of the G suit and the BLB mask, used by pilots to overcome problems of high altitude, and to significant inventions for diagnosing heart disorders.

1950   Doctors Edward Kendall and Philip Hench are awarded the Nobel Prize for isolation, identification, and synthesis of cortisone and application for treatment of arthritis.

1955   Mayo Clinic plays key role in development of open heart surgery.

1973   First medical center in the country to use CT scanning.

1985   Nonsurgical removal of gallstones is demonstrated.

1985   Computer-assisted stereotactic neurosurgery is conducted

The Mayo Properties Association, due to interest and need, became involved in the air transportation business. It established the Rochester Airport Company and subsidized airport construction. Lobb Field, located near old Highway 14, officially opened on July 13, 1928, when a Ford Tri-Motor plane landed on the sod runway. Regular passenger service to Chicago began the same year. No electric lights illuminated the runways. Instead flare pots, painstakingly filled with kerosene or diesel fuel each day, guided night-flying pilots.

Construction workers labored an entire year, from 1939 to 1940, paving runways and installing floodlights. In 1945 Mayo Clinic donated the airport to the city. During World War II many army planes—P-39s, P-63s, and P-47s—made regular stops in Rochester on their way to military bases in Alaska. Air traffic continued to increase and by 1950 a total of 56,000 passengers had landed in Rochester.

The present airport was completed in 1961. Only 250 people attended the morning dedication ceremonies, a disappointing turnout attributed to overcast skies. Northwest Airlines pilots practiced touch-and-go landings on the new, elongated runways, according to the August 19, 1961, issue of the *Rochester Post-Bulletin.* Like the sodbusters before them, passengers began pouring into Rochester. A total of 247,000 passengers landed here during 1969; many of them were Mayo Clinic patients.

Mayo Foundation's involvement with the airport continues. The city of Rochester contracted with the Rochester Airport Company to manage the operation of the airport and its facilities.

Mayo Clinic achieved worldwide fame due, in part, to its incorporation as a public foundation, pursuit of excellence, ongoing teaching programs, and long-range planning. Perhaps Louise Mayo's words explain the clinic's success best: "I think that the secret of The Doctor's usefulness was that he never looked backward. Looking backward is not a good thing for one's soul."

3

WAVES OF GRAIN

Rochester sits in a valley surrounded by bluffs, described in an 1876 geological survey as remarkable and level. Because glaciers did not move this far south, area soil remained free of the debris—massive boulders and thousands of small rocks—which usually accumulates in an outwash plain. "Bowlders [sic] are entirely absent in most parts of the county," noted geologist N.H. Winchell.

Loess soil, a rich, fine-grained, yellowish-brown loam, was deposited by the wind. This fertile topsoil proved to be good for farming. Sedimentary rock beneath the soil provided farmers with a natural drainage system. Water seeped through the soil and slowly filtered through layers of limestone. The result was soil with a fairly neutral pH rating, considered generally good for crop growth.

"If weeds will grow, so will wheat," speculated one Rochester farmer. Other farmers concurred and gradually turned from raising food for their families to raising cash crops. Minnesota's agricultural history can be divided into three time periods. In the first period, between 1850 and 1870, subsistence crops were raised. In the second period, from 1870 to 1895, wheat became king. And in the third period, from 1895 to the present, agriculture became diversified.

Joseph Stoppel and his brother George were typical of the hardworking farmers who settled in Rochester. Neither brother was trained in farming. Joseph was a bricklayer and stonemason; George was a cooper by trade. Accompanied by their families the brothers traveled to Rochester by oxcart in 1856. They staked claims on an elongated hillside approximately three miles west of the city. To file their claims the brothers walked to the nearest land office in La Crosse, Wisconsin, where they paid $1.25 an acre for their land, the average price.

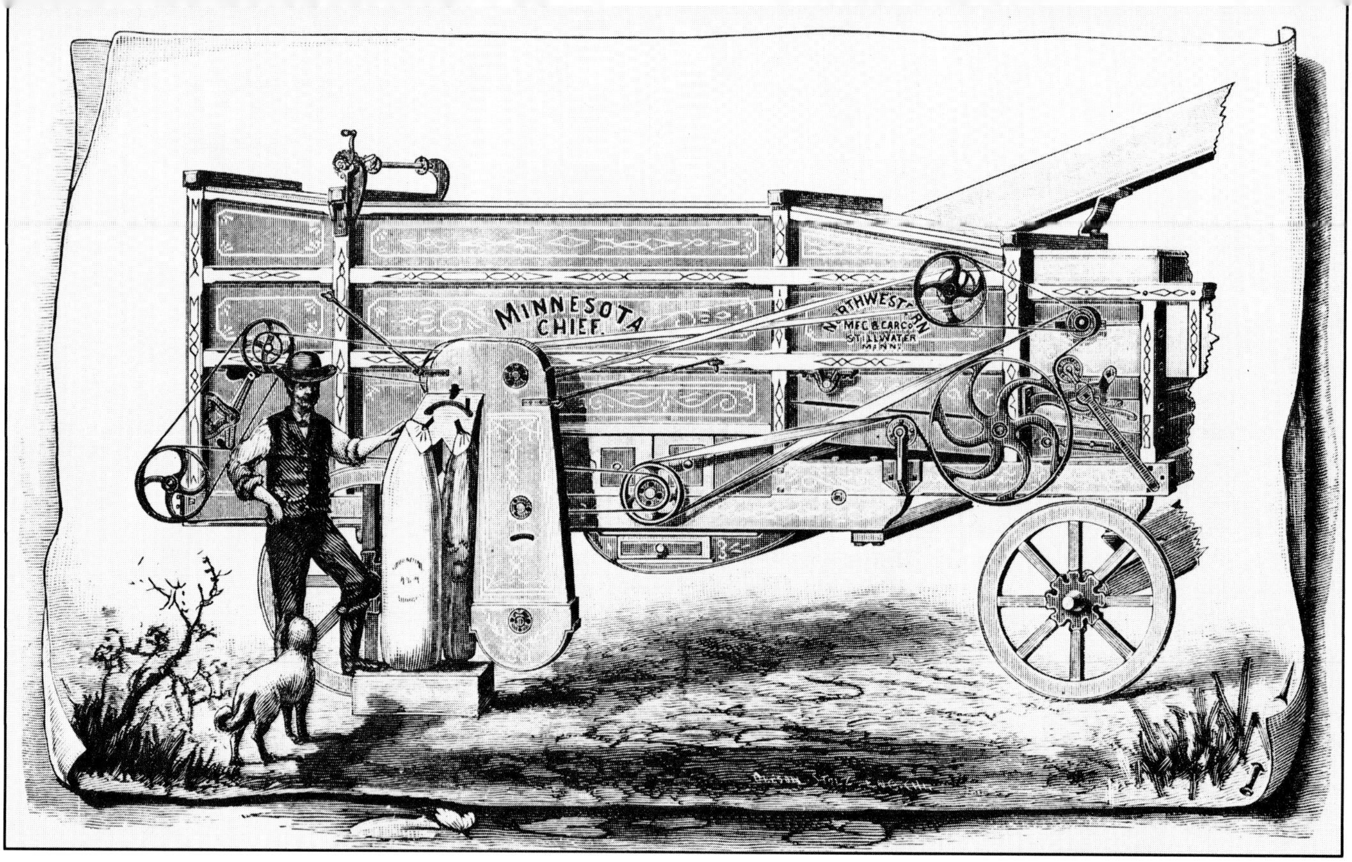

Above: This drawing of the Minnesota Sacking Chief appeared in the North-western Manufacturing and Car Company Catalog, *published in 1887. The catalog claimed: "men who buy a thresher to talk about may buy some cheap or gaudy affair; but those that buy one to use and earn big money will buy a Chief every time." Courtesy, Olmsted County Historical Society*

Right: George Stoppel married Mary Faber on December 25, 1849. The couple had four children: Louise, George Jr., Louisa, and Fred. One child died in the diphtheria epidemic of 1867. Courtesy, Olmsted County Historical Society

Far right: George Stoppel emmigrated from Germany in 1849, surviving 41 days on a sailing vessel. He went to Rochester, New York, first, where he farmed for one year. Ten years after his stone house was completed, Stoppel purchased a additional 80 acres of farmland. Stoppel held several Olmsted County offices. Courtesy, Olmsted County Historical Society

In compliance with government regulations, homesteaders could not claim more than a quarter section of land, or 160 acres. They were also required to build some sort of house, with minimum dimensions of 12 feet by 12 feet. With little time to build a cabin, George hollowed out a cave on the east side of the hill, where the family spent the winter.

When the weather turned warmer George began construction of a cabin near the entrance of the cave. The family lived in the cabin for two years while George built the family's permanent home, a traditional German house.

Stones for the house were quarried from a nearby hillside. An equally rugged barn was built near the house. Generations later, after the Stoppel farm had been acquired by the Olmsted County Historical Society, a restorer working on the barn commented it was "built like a cathedral."

George planted subsistence crops first, followed by potatoes, hay, and corn. The 1880 Agricultural Census listed the total area of the Stoppel farm at 150 acres. Fifty-five of these acres were grasslands and 35 acres remained as woodlands.

Attempting to lure farmers to the area, the Rochester Board of Trade publicized crop yields. The board cleverly used the poorest crop—potatoes—as an example. At an average of 95 bushels per acre, Rochester potato yields were higher than those of Vermont, New York, Virginia, Michigan, Iowa, New Hampshire, Massachusetts, Pennsylvania, Ohio, and Wisconsin. "One potato patch of 50 acres, after 27 successive crops, 25 of which were wheat, without fertilizing, gave a little over 12,000 bushels or a mean average of 240 bushels per acre," reported the Board of Trade. The sales pitch closed with the rhetorical question, "Can we grow potatoes?"

The Irish potato, relatively easy to grow, was the primary crop in Minnesota during the 1850s and early 1860s. Rochester farmers planted their share of potatoes, clearing the land with primitive hand tools: pickax, mattock, shovel, spade, grub hoe, and field hoe. These tools allowed farmers to plant around large trees or tree stumps.

Land was leveled with crude harrows made of tree branches, which had wooden pegs pounded into them, or with hand-hewn harrows made from massive beams. (Peg-tooth and spring-tooth harrows were developed later.) Furrows were made with ox-drawn wooden plows. Potato cuttings, each containing several "eyes," were planted, an exhausting form of stoop labor. Thus, farmers cheered the invention of the potato planter, a long-handled tool equipped with a foot lever which released cuttings into the soil.

Virgin soil was usually reserved for corn. According to Edward Lettermann, author of *Farming in Early Minnesota,* corn could be cultivated more easily on poorly cleared land. Corn did not require as fine a seedbed as other grains and could be harvested without large machinery. Like the potato farmers, corn farmers were rescued from stoop labor by the invention of the stab planter. Gravity did much of the work. When the two handles of the V-shaped tool were brought together, corn kernels, stored in a chamber on one side of the tool, rolled down the tube into the soil.

Corn was grown mainly to feed livestock. Rochester farmers harvested 23,063 bushels of corn in 1878. Other crop yields that year included 7,795 bushels of potatoes, 42,250 bushels of oats, 12,821 bushels of barley, and 157 bushels of buckwheat. Wheat had the highest yield at 165,860 bushels. Although weather certainly affected yields, the invention of the reaper revolutionized local agriculture.

Martha Stoppel holds an apple in her hands as she stands beside her cousins. One cousin sits cheerfully atop a manure spreader. Courtesy, Olmsted County Historical Society

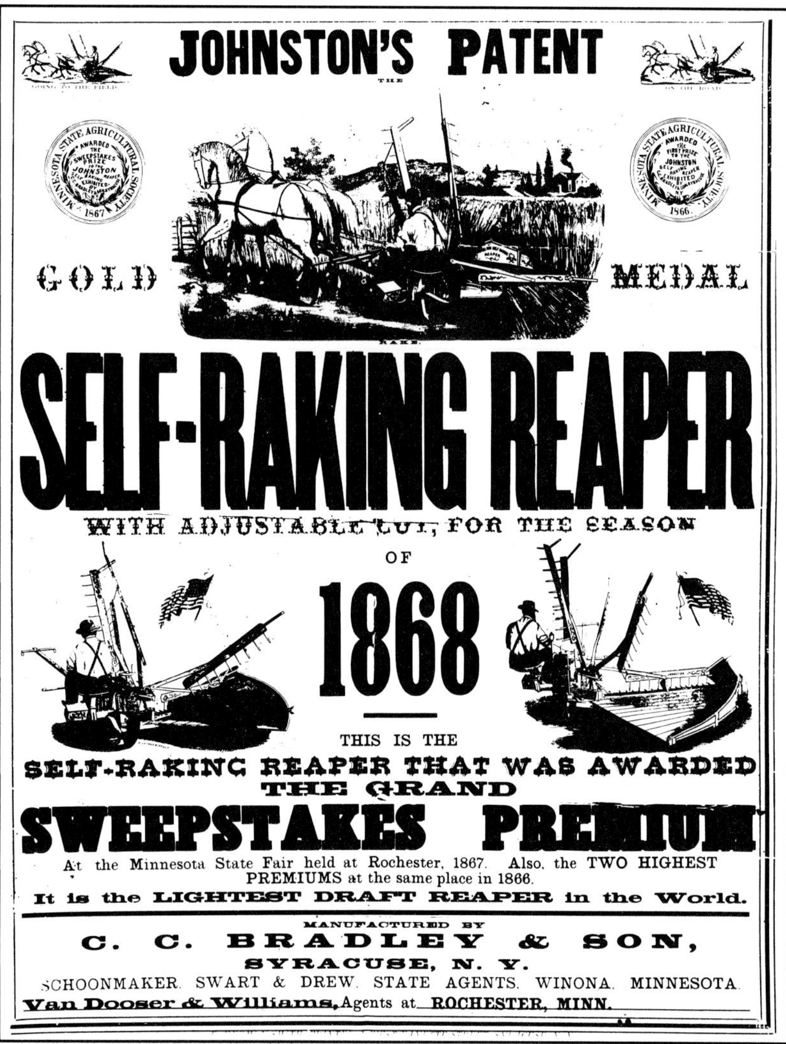

Self-raking reapers were a vast improvement over the original horse rakes, which forced the horse to stop every 2-3 seconds to discharge the load. Johnston's patented self-raking reaper was awarded the grand sweepstakes premium at the Minnesota State Fair, held in Rochester in 1867. Courtesy, Olmsted County Historical Society

Farm reapers reached Minnesota in 1855. "It was, however, after the outbreak of the Civil War, which drained away from the fields so much of the labor force, that the agricultural revolution began in earnest—a revolution not less striking and far-reaching in its effects than the industrial revolution which started in England a century earlier," noted Dr. Edward Van Dyke Robinson of the University of Minnesota.

Area farmers benefited from programs sponsored by the Farmer's Institute. Founded by Oren Gregg, a would-be minister turned farmer, these programs were the result of Gregg's lifelong commitment to agriculture. Gregg and his wife, Charlotte, turned their Lyon County home-stead into a model farm. Gregg theorized that overreliance on wheat farming would ultimately ruin soil, resulting in crop failure. So Gregg began experimenting with fertilizers and crop rotation. He pursued year-round dairy farming, feeding his cows a mixture of grain and cultivated hay. Officials of the Winona and St. Peter Railroad learned about Gregg's research, and in return for agricultural presentations they provided him with a railroad pass and paid other expenses. The Farmer's Institute was born.

With the zeal that would have gone into sermons, Gregg planned a variety of educational meetings for farmers. He worked hard to capture the public's attention, staging demonstrations, organizing meetings, and eventually establishing cooking schools for farmers' wives. Gregg's meetings were so successful that the 1887 Minnesota legislature appropriated $7,500 a year for statewide meetings and appointed Gregg as the salaried director of the Farmer's Institute.

The Olmsted County Farmer's Institute approved its bylaws at a March 1880 meeting. According to the bylaws the purpose of the institute was dissemination of information about farms, gardens, orchards, dairies, and apiaries. Anyone who wanted to join the institute could do so by paying 25 cents. Meetings were to be held on the first Thursday of every month.

"A more intelligent audience than daily attended the institute is seldom seen, and all appeared greatly interested and pleased with the work, charts, lectures, etc.," reported an article in the *Record & Union* in February 1890. The report gave details of a presentation on hogs by Mr. Louis, which included tips on feeding piglets. Louis explained he weaned his piglets at three months and substituted steamed food. A thorough man, Louis even told his audience what to do with hog manure.

If the invention of the reaper changed Rochester agriculture, so did the invention of the steam-powered threshing machine. Steam-powered threshers enabled farmers to process approximately 800 bushels of wheat a day. By the 1870s threshers were equipped with loading elevators which channeled grain into waiting wagons. But these labor-saving modifications also proved to be dangerous.

Flying sparks from the engine smokestack were a continuous hazard; any straw or flammable material close to the thresher could easily ignite. Farmers fueled the steam engine with scrap wood, old fenceposts, or chunks from the wood pile, which only added to the shower of sparks. Besides the threat of fire there was the threat of explosion. During a single year, 1911, it was estimated that two thresher explosions occurred daily in the United States.

On September 3, 1865, a notice in the *Rochester Post* warned threshers to comply with Session Laws, which prohibited running any threshing machine unless knuckles on the tumbling rod were properly and securely covered. Law violators would be denied their wages. "This is a good law and will tend to prevent accidents that occur to the peril of life and limb during the threshing season," the notice concluded. However, many farmers still were injured or killed.

Threshing bees became common. Farm wives rose at 3 A.M. to begin cooking the five hefty meals served to the threshing crew. Before chowing down platters of fried chicken, mountains of mashed potatoes, a variety of vegetables, and a choice of pies, crew members were required to clean up at the wash bench. The work was so hard and the food was so good that threshers tended to overeat,

Steam threshing crews were comprised of 15-25 men and included a separator man, sack-sewer, sack-jig man, strawbuck, loader, and roustabouts. The threshing machines had colorful names such as Red River, Advance Rumley, and Pride of Washington. Courtesy, Olmsted County Historical Society

PERMIT FOR STEAM THRESHING.

Permission is only granted under the following terms and conditions, and it is also understood and agreed that the following requirements shall be observed on the part of the insured, viz:

1st. Smoking is not allowed within TEN RODS from the threshing machine, and stack or straw.

2d. While there is fire in the furnace of the engine, it shall not be located within THIRTY FEET of any building or stack, and no COMBUSTIBLE LITTER OR STRAW shall be allowed to remain within FIFTEEN FEET of the furnace.

3d. A Screen of Wire, in perfect order, and of the best kind for arresting sparks, shall constantly and completely cover the top of the smoke stack; a competent WATCHMAN shall be in constant attendance upon the furnace, and at least ONE BARREL, full of water and ready for use, shall be kept within FIFTEEN FEET of the furnace.

4th. The boiler and furnace shall be in good condition, and furnished with all modern appliances for safety against fire.

5th. The engine shall not be run when the wind is blowing high from the furnace towards the stacks or buildings.

6th. During the absence of the persons engaged in threshing, a trustworthy WATCHMAN shall be left in attendance until all the fire is extinguished.

Violation of any of these conditions will render this policy absolutely void.

Attached to Policy No. *654 x 826 c* of the Rochester Farmers Mutual Fire Insurance Company.

Issued to *R. L. Cotterell* *J. Schmelzer*, Secretary. Rochester, Minn. *July 31 the* 189*1*. *J. M. Duell*, President.

This permit was issued to Richard Lloyd Cotterell, a native of Worcestershire, England, who arrived in Rochester in June 1856. Cotterell earned his reputation as a fruit grower. The 1883 History of Olmsted County, Minnesota *reported: "Mr. Cotterell is engaged largely in fruit raising and has the finest apple orchard in the county." Courtesy, Olmsted County Historical Society*

which led to the colloquialism "eat like a bunch of threshers."

Wheat became king, and crew members worked exhaustive days during the wheat harvest. High demand and short supply during the Civil War years pushed wheat prices upward. Rochester farmers responded by planting more wheat. "Wheat was in demand the world over. It was storable, exportable, and essentially a food for people," explained Paul Johnson, in *Farm Inventions in the Making of America.* Wheat could also be sown in fall or spring.

An 1860 news article congratulated county farmers on their steadily rising wheat production. Yields were listed at 28 bushels per acre, with a mean average of 20 bushels, a production level exceeded only by Chisago County. Moreover, Olmsted County was cited as one of the four fastest growing wheat counties in the state. Immigrants were advised to take notice of this fact.

" Olmsted County the Center of the Finest Grain Producing Country in the World," heralded a headline in the November 16, 1861, issue of the *Rochester City Post.* This grandiose claim was based on a survey of southeastern Minnesota counties taken by the Commissioner of Statistics. The article concluded "Olmsted, being in the very heart of this section . . . must be set down as the banner Agricultural County in a State which stands forth pre-eminently as the finest grain-producing section, in the whole world!"

Twelve years later Olmsted County had the highest grain harvest in the history of the state. High grain yields of oats, corn, barley, flax, and wheat were attributed to favorable weather and a sustained growing season. "Never, in the history of the state, have the labors of a husbandman been more richly rewarded," wrote one reporter.

Farmers relied on the railroad to transport these grains to market. Responding to the farmers' needs, gandy dancers (workmen who pounded railroad track into position) laid track as fast as possible. In 1862 only 10 miles of track had been laid in the state. Ten years later over 1,900 miles of track crisscrossed the state. Villages erupted along railroad routes and attracted new, profit-seeking settlers. "Each individual was a speculator in the wildest sense of the term," observed Philip Harris of the Lake Superior and Mississippi Railroad. Many of the wheat buyers were agents employed by the railroads.

Yet not all Rochester grain was shipped to central collection points. Some grain went directly to the Union Brewery, established in 1858. Henry Schuster bought the brewery in 1865, only to have the plant burn down several years later. Schuster rebuilt the brewery and increased its production capacity. Six thousand barrels of beer, plus 300,000 bottles of beer, were manufactured in 1895. Either Schuster knew beer or Rochester residents were terribly thirsty—no matter. The *Rochester Daily Post* (souvenir edition) declared Schuster's beer was best, "the verdict of discriminating judges."

The future of wheat farming seemed unlimited. Flushed with success, wheat farmers overextended themselves. "The farmers went wheat mad," wrote Helen Clapesattle. "They claimed more land, bought more machines, planted more wheat, more, and more." Wheat prices fluctuated for a time. But in 1869 wheat dropped from two dollars a bushel to 60 cents a bushel, then to 50 cents a bushel, and finally to the all-time low, 40 cents a bushel.

Prices took such a dive in August of 1872 that the *Federal Union* commented, "This has undoubtedly made some men poorer than they were." The next year prices dropped again. Decline was attributed to oversupply, a falling dollar, public panic, and high railroad freight rates—at least, rates that were high in comparison to the market price of wheat.

Besides economic disasters farmers grappled with natural disasters. As early

Since Lyman Tondro owned the Cascade Mills, he had his name printed on each flour sack. The graham flour in this sack was used to make rather heavy muffins and bread. Courtesy, Olmsted County Historical Society

In order to publicize its Malt and Hop Tonic, Schuster's Brewery had these austere postcards printed. Hops were used to flavor malt liquors and, according to the 1894 supplement to the Encyclopedia Britannica, had narcotic and sedative properties. Courtesy, Olmsted County Historical Society

as 1863 the *Rochester City Post* was reporting drought conditions. "Unless rain soon falls, an actual [crop] elimination to the state must come," reported the newspaper. Drought conditions were reported as being worse in northern counties. The Mississippi River was at its lowest point in 15 years. "Nothing but a reasonable and thorough rain can avert the failure of crops in the state," the report concluded. For a decade, from 1887 to 1897, the plains states were plagued by drought conditions.

Farmers also contended with grasshopper swarms. In 1874 grasshoppers were sighted near New Ulm. Eyewitnesses reported seeing so many insects that "the earth and the heavens filled with them." The six- to eight-mile-wide column of grasshoppers, rising an estimated 40 feet into the air, finally reached Rochester. Countless acres of farmland were devoured.

Concerned citizens met at the courthouse to plan relief efforts. Officers were elected and placed a notice in the newspaper, asking for donations of money and supplies. "There has never been a more deserving cause than this, nor one that should meet with a more ready response from the entire community," noted the *Rochester Post.*

Drought and pestilence forced farmers to consider preventive measures such as crop diversification. G.F. Seiler took diversification to heart. He planted 16 acres of broom corn on his farm, located two miles west of the city. From this acreage Seiler manufactured a whopping 6,500 brooms. His experiment proved so successful that he planted 20 acres the next year and made broom corn his specialty.

Other crops, such as flax, were introduced as well. Flax production began in 1895. The *Rochester Daily Post,* in a May 8, 1896, article, hailed the crop as an industrial institution designed to assume gigantic proportions. This assumption was based on the newly patented flax brake and scutching machine invented by Rochester resident Alexander Morrison. "It is the only machine of the kind in existence," stated the article.

Morrison's invention mechanically separated flax fibers from the woody parts of the plant. "One man, with the assistance of two boys, will be enabled to turn out a ton of fibre every day," predicted the *Daily* reporter. Flax growers, anticipating big profits, imported enough seed from Belgium to plant 135 acres.

Walworth, Hubbard & Company of Chicago offered to put up flax dressing machinery "wherever the amount available will warrant it." Payment to farmers was listed as $6 to $8 per ton for tangled or rotted straw and $7 to $10 per ton for straight straw. To qualify for payment, flax growers had to deliver their product to stations along Chicago railroad lines. H.R. Jones, a local flax grower, advised farmers to "Save your crop carefully, and though the drouth has shortened the straw it is valuable as it is, if the fibre is only good."

But it was dairy farming and not flax that became Rochester's major industry—surprising since dairying was more complex, requiring investment capital, buildings, fenced acreages, high-quality feeds, cooperative weather, and efficient collection points. Dairy herds increased to such an extent that the newspaper introduced a regular column entitled "Creamery Interests."

When ice prices rose sharply the column advised dairy farmers to build cooperative icehouses. "The outlay of money and time will then be very small, and the real cost of ice in the summer months practically nothing," explained the column writer. Essentials for an efficient icehouse were listed: sawdust packing, double light-colored walls (to reflect the sun), a slanted roof, and good drainage. Dairymen were also advised not to make butter from frozen milk, which would cause it to become crumbly and bitter, and to salt butter in the churn, one pound of salt for each 10 pounds of butter.

The writer of "Creamery Interests" in a November 28, 1890, column exhorted readers, "Do not be afraid of pure, wholesome milk as an everyday diet, because

it is a virgin drink, an elixir of life to babes, and a brawn producer to adults." Dairy farmers were cautioned not to expect pure and wholesome milk unless they monitored sanitation including stable drainage, maintained adequate drinking facilities, kept animals free from bovine diseases, and provided healthy feed.

Development of the dairy industry hinged upon the efforts of Dr. Charles Mayo, who had been selected chairman of the city council. One of his chief concerns was the contamination of Rochester milk, which was so tainted one inspector rated it the dirtiest in the state among cities of comparable size. Overriding the mayor's veto, Dr. Charlie persuaded the city council to pass dairy inspection laws. These laws required dairy farmers to wash their hands with antiseptic soap, wear spotlessly clean clothes, handle milk in cooling rooms, and pasteurize all milk.

In addition, Dr. Charlie established an experimental dairy at Mayowood, which he later incorporated with another dairyman, James Punderson, to form the

Mayowood Farm Dairy. Mule wagons delivered milk from Mayowood to 38 customers. And in 1925 the Supremacy Dairy joined forces with the Mayowood Farm Dairy to form the Rochester Dairy Company.

World War II increased the demand for milk and Rochester dairy farmers responded to it. The Rochester Dairy cooperative was created in 1942 to meet this demand. A $200,000 milk processing plant was constructed on land secured from the Chicago Great Western Railroad. Plant workers raced to perfect dehydrated milk production. Recalled one Rochester resident, "The milk was as dark as cocoa and terribly difficult to hydrate."

Persistence paid off. Powdered milk manufactured in the cooperative's drying room was sold to the U.S. government for school lunch programs and the armed forces. Ice cream mix, a by-product of powdered milk, was packaged in five-gallon containers lined with polyethylene. Designed in cooperation with Hoerner Boxes, Inc., of Keokuk, Iowa, the

The Supremacy Dairy merged with Mayowood Farm Dairy in 1925 to form the Rochester Dairy. The dairy was located in the former Schuster Brewery. Here early morning milk trucks are parked at the rear entrance of the dairy. Courtesy, Olmsted County Historical Society.

The Rochester Geese

Rochester loves its geese. Geese have been incorporated into logos, products, crafts, even the city flag. Visitors consider seeing the geese a must, photographing them and feeding them corn kernels or bread crusts. According to a count taken in 1982, over 30,000 geese make Silver Lake their home.

Silver Lake is an artificial lake, located on the previous site of Silver Lake millpond and scrap land composed of sand deposits and scruffy woods. Built during the 1930s, the $500,000 project was partly funded by the Works Progress Administration (WPA). Eight hundred workers, whose wages were $40 a month, sloshed through mud and snow to clear the land with mule-drawn scrapers. In 1948 a dam was built to provide a cooling pond for the city power plant. This warm, ice-free water attracted migrating geese and many remained in Rochester year-round.

Dr. Charles Mayo began raising geese at Mayowood in 1924. The site attracted more geese until there were several hundred at Mayowood and Silver Lake. By 1940 the flock had grown to 4,000. The flock increased in 1947 when a grateful Mayo Clinic patient donated 12 Nebraska geese to the existing flock.

In 1962 wildlife experts identified the geese as *Branta canadensis maximia,* or giant Canadian geese, a subspecies thought to be extinct. The primary difference between the giant Canadian and other geese is size. Giant Canadas weigh from 12 to 14 pounds, as compared to the average 8-pound weight of other species. Commensurate with size is the larger wingspan of the geese, which ranges from 69 to 71 inches.

Rochester views these geese as special guests. "Not that everyone always loves the guests. Some see them as polluting, noisy intruders whose numbers are much too large," wrote *Rochester Post-*

Just before sunset thousands of geese, sated with corn gleaned from outlying fields, fly home to Silver Lake for the night. Photo by Gary Koenig

new lightweight container was given an award by the military.

The Rochester Dairy product line expanded to include grade "A" pasteurized milk and cream, ice cream, butter, cottage cheese, and bulk condensed milk for bakers, candy, and ice cream manufacturers. This cooperative evolved into the present-day Associated Milk Producers Incorporated (AMPI).

Those farmers not interested in dairying experimented with other crops. Oats thrived in local soil. "Statistics Show That Olmsted County Produces More Oats Than the Whole State of West Virginia," announced a headline in the November 13, 1891, issue of the *Rochester Post.* Other farmers grew apples, raspberries, strawberries, and plums, with yields described as immense. Residents who recalled the history of the state horticultural society must have been stunned.

The Minnesota Horticultural Society was founded in Rochester in 1866. Its primary purpose was improvement of horticulture, rural adornment, and landscape gardening. Articles of incorporation levied one dollar as a yearly membership fee, issued stock privileges, listed officers, and stipulated that meeting locations would be determined by the society.

One of the horticultural society's first concerns was whether apples could be raised in Rochester. Members decided to compile a list of hardy varieties of fruit and recommended cultivation of small fruits that could be raised in abundance. Addressing an 1878 meeting of the society, Judge Burt Eaton said, "Our horticultur-

Bulletin staff writer John Weiss. But three public opinion polls, conducted over a 10-year period, reveal that most Rochester residents think the geese are an asset.

Residents and visitors alike consider the geese *our* geese. Seeing these huge birds flying in V-formation and hearing them honking as they skim treetops makes observers feel close to nature. Radio commentator Paul Harvey devoted part of his December 28, 1987, broadcast to Rochester's geese. Harvey called the geese "stately creatures" and reported there was no vandalism or vicious killings of the birds.

Explained Harvey, "It has to do with the traditional hospitable character of the people of this medical mecca, for Rochester, as you know, is also home of the Mayo Clinic, where couples of all ages have come to relearn how to hold hands and the city has learned to welcome all visitors with a gentle embrace. Dear hearts and gentle people, thank you for taking care of our geese."

ists, profiting by experience, and acquiring a knowledge through patient, intelligent investigation and effort, will demonstrate to us today that apples, fine, fair, and luscious, can be successfully grown in Minnesota."

Judge Eaton castigated unscrupulous suppliers who shipped apple growers dead or damaged trees, "as dead as last year's brush heap." Predicted Judge Eaton, "Your good sense and sagacity will not permit you to hesitate long in adopting the varieties which promise largest success." His prediction came true. Today the Hiawatha area, which includes Rochester, is the second-largest producer of Haralson apples in the state.

The introduction of county fairs gave farmers an opportunity to share their stories and display their products. The first county fair was organized in 1860. Sponsored by the Olmsted County Agricultural Society, the fair was held on land now known as Soldiers Field. Membership in the society cost 50 cents, a fee which included exhibition privileges and free admission for exhibitors' families.

With the exception of the Civil War years, county fairs were held throughout the 1860s. These fairs became so popular that state fairs were also held in Rochester in 1866, 1867, 1869, 1880, 1881, and 1882. Unlike today's fairs these were celebrations of a simple, rural life-style. No carnival rides. No demolition derbies. No junk food. Just simple entertainment.

The 1885 fair was the first to be illuminated by electricity. Electric lights must have paled in comparison to the fair's publicity stunt, a wedding contest. Fair officials accepted applications from

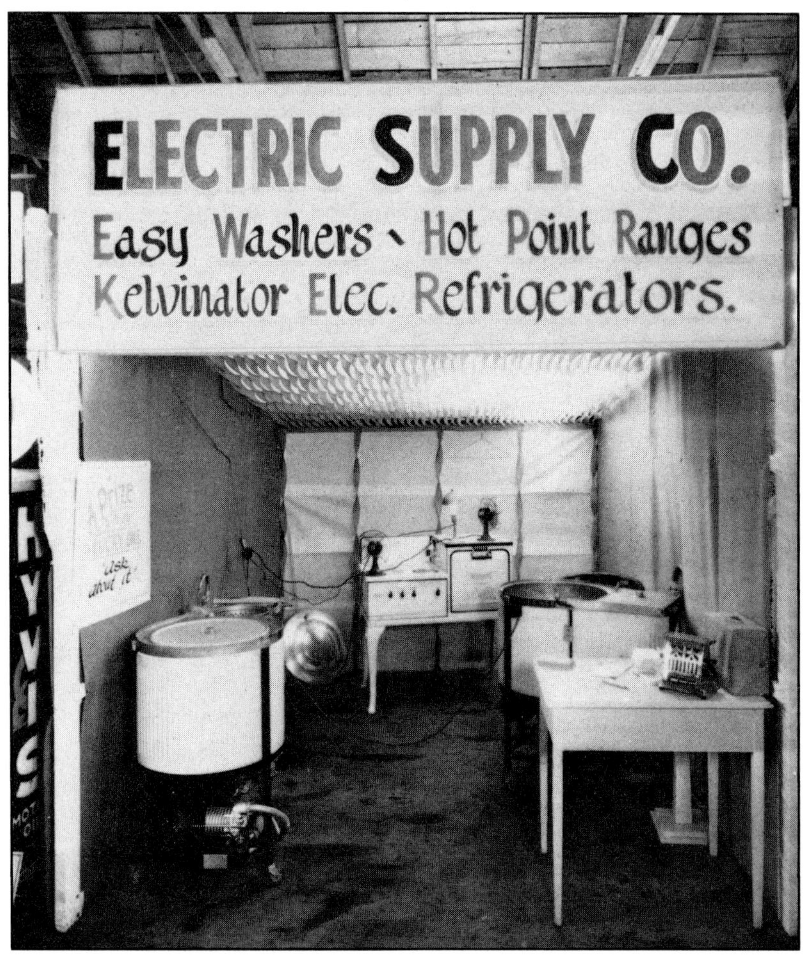

George Morrison owned the Electric Supply Company and displayed his wares at the 1925 county fair. For unknown reasons, the Electric Supply Company failed in 1931. Courtesy, Olmsted County Historical Society

"Candidates for Matrimonial Happiness." Thomas Elford and his fiancée, Adline Postier, were selected as contest winners. Businesses closed and church bells pealed during the wedding, which was held on the fairgrounds. The bride and groom received prizes from local merchants, including a Garland cookstove, 25 yards of Brussels carpet, and a rocking chair.

The 1896 county fair made local fame because of a horse race. Two Rochester horses, Kitty Myers and Sleepy David, were pitted against each other. Sleepy David, an old horse, was aptly named. He started the race well, but according to spectators, foundered because he was poorly ridden. With a final burst of speed Sleepy David neared the finish line, stumbled, and fell. The jockey jumped to safety, but Sleepy David was dead.

The first annual exhibition of the Southern Minnesota Poultry and Pet Stock Association was held at Library Hall in 1884. Local merchants donated the fair prizes. Special premiums were also awarded for "anything in the way of pets, such as Canary Birds, Mocking Birds, Gold Fish, Squirrels, Foxes, etc., etc." The Singer Manufacturing company gave $1.50 to the winner of the best white-crested black Polish cock—exotic sounding, to say the least.

When emphasis shifted from county fairs to school displays, the Southern Minnesota Fair Association disbanded. In 1900 grounds and buildings were sold at a public auction for $6,425. Twelve years later the fair concept was revived by Dr. Christopher Graham, who donated 160 acres of land including buildings, valued at $25,000, to the association.

The 4-H clubs merged with the Olmsted County Fair Association in 1931. Boys and Girls clubs were the forerunners of 4-H. A.F. Borchert, author of the first Olmsted County extension report, described the work of the clubs, particularly the "considerable interest in the calf-feeding contest." Borchert also noted that the winning pig gained 1.89 pounds a day over 100 days. These clubs were basically one-project clubs, focusing on livestock for boys and canning for girls.

Founded in 1925, 4-H clubs differed from the earlier Boys and Girls clubs in two ways. First, membership was open to both sexes. Second, members could work on a variety of projects. The Rochester club had 22 members in 1931. Many surrounding communities started 4-H clubs. The clubs continued to prosper and by 1935 there were 17 clubs in Olmsted County; membership surged to 539. Club projects ranged from livestock judging to accounting.

Although farmers and farm-related groups were aware that soil could be misused, generations passed before conservation measures were publicly accepted. "We claim our soil to be practically inexhaustible," declared the 1884 Rochester Board of Trade. This attitude, coupled with poor planting methods, resulted in the Dust Bowl years, which lasted from 1932 to 1940. During this time farmers battled two enemies—weather and low grain prices.

Desperate farmers sought reform through the National Grange of the Patrons of Husbandry groups, more commonly known as the Grange. The movement was founded in 1867 by Oliver Hudson Kelley, who had farmed in Minnesota. Within five years there were 540 branches of the Grange throughout the state. "The movement has been fraught with many beneficial results to farmers," reported the 1874 *Andreas Atlas*.

The Grange was a radical group for its time. Female members and children, once they turned 14, had the right to vote. John Schelbecker, author of *Whereby We Thrive: A History of American Farming, 1607-1972*, attributed much of the Grange's success to timing. "The solutions they advocated usually would not have produced the desired results," he noted. The Grange was instrumental in securing legislation, most notably the Granger Laws that designated railroads a public utility, a decision upheld by the Supreme Court in 1876.

Local branches of the Grange, however, failed to achieve prosperity for Rochester farmers. The problems they faced were far more complex than railroad freight rates and interstate commerce. Economic reform, particularly of banking laws, was sorely needed. Political—and some say religious—entanglements undermined the Grange movement. Farmers and businessmen alike turned their thoughts to economic expansion.

World War II provided impetus not only for dairy farmers, but also for crop farmers who rallied to increase food production. The use of insecticides and fertilizers became standard farm practice. Because of "the great war-born demand for agricultural products and the relatively high level of farm income," use of phosphates reached an all-time peak in 1946 according to W.H. Pierre in *The Yearbook of Agriculture: 1943-1947*.

Farmers also relied on nitrogen fertilizers, which were absorbed into the soil

Fulkerson's Grocery Store, located on South Broadway, advertised regularly in The Record and Union. *Courtesy, Olmsted County Historical Society*

along with other fertilizers or applied as a side-dressing after crops were well established. Among orchard growers, use of lead arsenate as an insecticide became standard, but the poisonous substance often injured trees and accumulated in the soil. DDT became a common pesticide but eventually proved to be harmful to beneficial insects, besides leaving a residue.

DDT, lead arsenate, nitrogen fertilizers, and phosphates proved to be precursors to the groundwater crisis of the 1980s. "Balance is a fundamental part of nature's law," wrote C.B. Shear and H.L. Crane in *The Yearbook of Agriculture*. "But man's activities have a way of upsetting nature's balance and usually it takes a serious unbalance to make us see the situation and try to correct it."

After the war agricultural and economic changes were needed. Perhaps recalling the now infamous 1884 Rochester Board of Trade, farmers and businessmen turned their thoughts to economic expansion. As the Board of Trade said, "Honest industry in any branch of business, particularly the line of manufactures, will surely meet with a grand success in Rochester, as the market for most manufactured goods is provided near at hand, and the profits are large."

Board members never imagined their economic dreams would lead to computers amidst the corn rows.

This IBM worker assembles
the first collator manufactured in Rochester. Courtesy,
IBM

4

COMPUTERS AMIDST THE CORN ROWS

Around 1892 the Rochester Woolen Mills posted long handbills all over town. The headline, printed in capital letters, seemed to scream at the public: "A SAFE EIGHT PER CENT. INVESTMENT." Actually, the handbill was more of an essay, a wordy appeal to prospective investors, urging them to purchase shares in the mill at $20 each. The opening paragraph was persuasive copy:

It is now generally conceded that all new Textile Mills in this country will be located nearer to where the raw material is produced—the Cotton Mills in the cotton fields of the South, and the Woolen Mills adjacent to the sheep ranges of the great Northwest, where millions of pounds of wool are produced. The skilled workmen will follow the Mills, and the local unemployed population will be brought in and gradually instructed in business.

A.G. Sells had a lawyer draw up a legal agreement between himself, as entrepreneur, and the citizens of Rochester. Dated March 3, 1892, the document proposed that citizens assist Sells in financing a local woolen mill through stock sales, raising no less than $20,000 in start-up capital. The proposal was based on the technology Sells had to offer, "being owner of some valuable improvement in knitting and hosiery."

Improvements were cited as woolen cards, spinning frame, wool picker, card grinder, yarn scales, yarn twister, and 12 knitting machines. Sells' appeal was successful. "Rochester Woolen Mills Will Begin Operation at Once," reported the February 10, 1899, edition of the *Post & Record*. The factory contained a sorting room, sewing room, and trouser-pressing room. Newspaper advertisements pictured each of these rooms, spotlighting

During 1937 the Rochester Bottling Company, owned by Morton Emmons, manufactured 70,000 cases of carbonated drinks for delivery within a 35-mile radius of Rochester. Courtesy, Olmsted County Historical Society

the sewing room where "Minnesota girls made Rochester Cassimere [a cashmere fabric] trousers."

The Rochester Woolen Mills provided employment for 107 people. In addition, three traveling salesmen journeyed to nearby states to promote the woolen mill's expanding product line, which grew to include sweaters, scarves, and mittens. Equally important were the technological advances the Rochester Woolen Mills and other factories brought to Rochester.

Business flourished in Rochester. The city had no less than three cigar factories, all located downtown. Excelsior soap was also manufactured in Rochester. Blake & Company, whose owners may have longed for a warmer climate, manufactured palm-leaf hats. To make use of locally grown corn, Frank Spooner opened a broom factory in 1871. "This is a new industry in our city and we are glad to see it started," reported the *Rochester Post.* Mrs. E.M. Coon opened her candy factory at the corner of College and Eagle streets and advertised that her fresh candies were sold at Chicago prices.

Other manufacturers included a mineral water factory, glove factory, cheese factory (which used the milk of some 200 cows), tin works, bedspring factory, corset factory, marble works, iron works, and carriage factory. The factories did a brisk business. For example, Northwestern Wagon Works, manufacturers of buggies, phaetons, and double wagons, produced from 100 to 150 wagons a year. But the firm's 12 employees could not keep up with the rising demand for wagons, particularly the company's specialty, the Dexter.

Sales of the Success Washing Machine were boosted when the machine was awarded first premium at the Olmsted County Agricultural Fair. Owner Henry Huny advertised in the newspaper, "The subscriber desires to say to the housewives of Rochester and vicinity that he is manufacturing and keeps on hand for sale, the Success Washing Machine, an indespensible article in every household." Huny added that the machine had been thoroughly tested by several intelligent ladies and gentlemen.

On the corner of Broadway and Seventh Street, The Rochester Factory, Buttles & Herrick, proprietors, opened for business. The factory specialized in manufacturing furniture for homes, offices, and schools, as well as doors and window sashes. The cost of a transom sash was 75 cents. An entire set of wooden chairs, presumably four, could be purchased for $3.50.

Brickmaking, however, was the object of a humorous article in the May 24, 1876, issue of the *Record & Union*. A reporter wrote:

Richard Tilton has opened his mud foundry for the manufacture of brick, his principal mud hen being Frank Eddy, who when clad in his brick yard regimentals, makes no odds of Jack Falstaff or his motley recruits. What a picture, as he meanders through the yard, with the jib boom of his coat flying in ribbons to the wind, eyes distended, and his bare toes saying "wibble wabble," *as the soft mud looms up between them and gracefully folds itself over each.*

Local brickmakers worked diligently to increase production, and by 1869 they were turning out thousands of bricks. Henry Cross' brickyard manufactured 260,000 bricks that year. S. Stone's brickyard manufactured 250,000 bricks. And Whitcomb Brothers made a whopping one million bricks, over two-thirds of which were used for construction projects within city limits.

Surprisingly, the 1883 *History of Olmsted County, Minnesota* criticized area brickmakers: "Although the material is sandy, more sand is usually put in making the brick, which are consequently of poor quality." The writer's criticism was softened somewhat by the comment, "The brick vitrify little when burned."

Rochester also had its share of inventors, who applied their ingenuity to everything from shoe polish to piston rings. H. Knutsen invented (or improved upon) waterproof shoe polish for ladies. A local newspaper claimed the polish was beneficial in all kinds of weather since it did not penetrate the leather but provided a hard, protective surface.

A.T. Stebbins and C.W. Cresap joined forces to manufacture Cresap's invention, the knuckle joint oscillating bob sleigh.

Rochester Iron Works was located at the corner of Fourth and Oak streets. E. Chapman, W.M. Purvis, and F.D. Livermore were the proprietors. Run by Fred Livermore from 1873 to 1902, the company manufactured steam engines. Other products for sale included the Cyclone engine, boilers, well drilling tools, pulleys, iron and brass castings, pipes, and pipe fittings. Courtesy, Olmsted County Historical Society

In 1908 Henry Postier began his career as a chauffeur. He drove for Dr. Will and for the famous surgeon, Dr. Stevens Duryea. Around 1912 Postier went into business with Carl West. Their South Street garage repaired Burt Eaton's car, charging $4.25 for eight and one-half hours of Postier's labor. Courtesy, Olmsted County Historical Society

The partners opened their business in a former warehouse on East Fourth Street. This sleigh was special because "It is so constructed that upon striking an obstruction the runner merely oscillates on a joint and passes smoothly over instead of, as with ordinary bob, hitting and often overturning the entire sleigh," as reported in the *Olmsted County Democrat* on November 30, 1893.

G.A. Gregorson invented a new type of horse net and a machine to knit it. The horse net, which included triangular ear pieces, was draped over a horse to keep flies away. Most were decorated with tassels; some were multi-colored. Gregorson installed his knitting machine in his store and operated it himself. His invention caught the attention of the *Rochester Post*, which reported on May 11, 1883, that "We saw at his harness store a few days ago a simple and ingenious machine of his own invention."

The brief article did not divulge the price of Gregorson's horse nets, but they must have been cheap. The 1908 *Sears, Roebuck & Company Catalog* contained ads for cotton cord mesh horse nets (the cheapest) at 70 cents each, and special thru-row tassel tug nets (the most expensive) at $1.93. "We recommend to all our drivers of horses to use some kind of fly net on their horses during the fly season," said the catalog.

Another innovative Rochester resident, O.F. Buttles, invented a new type of windmill. Brooks & Clark agreed to manufacture the windmill, opened their factory, and launched an aggressive advertising campaign. The advertisements claimed, "We make a specialty of manufacturing and putting up the Buttles Wind Mill over the celebrated Traborn Underground Force Pump, and by laying pipe underground, water may be delivered at any height or distance from the fountain."

Later editions of the newspaper contained testimonials for the Buttles Wind Mill and referred to specific installations. One windmill was positioned over an especially deep well—305 feet—in Mazeppa. Besides windmills the company carried a variety of pumps: iron suction, lift, iron force, cistern force, pitcher spout, and wood, which was so unusual that an exclamation point appeared after the word. And farmers could purchase a Boss Sickle Grinder at the Brooks & Clark store for a mere $10.

Brooks & Clark perfected the art of manufacturing windmills, or so claimed a May 24, 1878, article in the *Record & Union.* The company improved upon But-

tles' original design and selected more rugged materials for the windmill's 10-foot wheel, with its 14 fans. Fans were affixed so that they "faced the wind in proportion to the speed required," concluded the article. Buttles also invented a special snowplow, with curved steel blades, for use on locomotives.

But it was Otto Haling's inventions that received worldwide attention. From boyhood Haling was an inveterate tinkerer. His high school shop-class project was a full-sized tractor. When the semester concluded, Otto drove the tractor home to the Haling farm in northwest Rochester, where it was used for years. "He always wanted to do something better," recalled Haling's wife, Hazel.

Haling rented space in a local chicken hatchery and opened a machine shop. Around 1933 he began work on his first invention, an improved piston ring. The vented steel ring was more durable than previous cast-iron rings. Next he began work on a machine to coil piston rings. In 1936 Haling completed his design. This specialized machine coiled piston rings at a rate eight times faster than human labor, producing as many as 20,000 rings a day.

Haling designed more than 100 inventions: a machine for making piston spac- ers, a machine that automatically bored and beveled cast-iron piston rings and valve seats, and a machine that bored the inside, top cast of iron compression rings. In 1963 thousands of ring segments, 50,000 to 750,000, were sold to piston ring companies.

Sadly, Haling's inventions were pirated by unscrupulous inventors and companies. "Invent a better mousetrap and thieves will find a way to your doorstep," mused Haling. His plain tube carburetor was pirated by a major farm-equipment manufacturer. His two-spindle automatic boring machine was pirated by a Swiss firm. His strip steel coils, produced on Haling's patented machine, were pirated by a toy company.

While visiting a factory that had purchased one of Haling's machines, an engineer became intrigued by the coils the machine produced and took a sample home. One of his children accidentally dropped the coil on the top step of the stairs. Amazingly, the coil alternately compressed, expanded, and "walked" down the stairs. A toy manufacturer spotted the coil's play potential and began production. Haling was out of roughly one million dollars.

Part of the fault was Haling's, and he knew it. Obsessed with inventing, Haling neglected to obtain the necessary interna-

Right: Otto Haling's career began in the early 1930s. After high school graduation, Haling decided to become an inventor. "One day I began to wonder about ways to improve a piston ring," recalled Haling. "I needed something to sell to the public and piston rings fit the bill perfectly." Courtesy, Mrs. Otto Haling

Facing page, top: Kerry and Fred Conley began manufacturing silent shutter cameras in their home town of Spring Valley during 1899. In 1904 Sears, Roebuck & Company approached the brothers about moving their factory to Rochester. The brothers went into partnership with James Drake and opened their factory on Fourth Street, where 25 employees assembled box cameras. Courtesy, Olmsted County Historical Society

Facing page, bottom: Between January 1942 and June 1943, the Waters Conley Company focused upon wartime production. This worker is operating a punch press machine. Courtesy, Olmsted County Historical Society

tional patents for some of his inventions or to follow through with marketing plans. "That's the way I am, spending more time inventing than I do making money," he explained. Haling sued some of his competitors but wound up with token compensation.

The team of Kerry and Fred Conley had better luck. In 1889 they started manufacturing cameras. Sears, Roebuck & Company purchased the business around 1920 and renamed it the Conley Camera Company. The factory manufactured cameras exclusively for Sears until Sears decided to purchase cameras from Eastman Company. The factory was then converted into a phonograph factory and began production of spring-wound players.

Glen M. Waters purchased the company and renamed it the Waters Conley Company. During World War II the company had a number of government contracts for top secret work. As subcontractors of Western Electric Company, the Waters Conley Company helped design and manufacture radar-guided missiles. Under another subcontract with the Minneapolis-based Honeywell Regular Company, Waters Conley developed an electronic gas gauge for aircraft. Four thou-

sand emergency fishing-tackle containers were also produced for the Army Air Corps.

Waters Conley received the Army-Navy "E" Award, presented for "unusual resourcefulness and devotion to duty." A red and blue "E" banner was flown proudly over the plant, alongside the red, white, and blue banners the company had received for the Minnesota governor's safety award, presented in 1944.

After World War II Waters Conley returned to manufacturing phonographs, this time amplified portables. Sears, Roebuck & Company again became primary purchasers of these phonographs in 1949. With the introduction of long-playing, high-fidelity records in the 1950s, phonograph production soared. In 1953 Waters Conley manufactured an all-time high of 184,000 phonographs, sold through Sears outlets under the Silvertone label.

Despite high phonograph sales Waters Conley realized it had to diversify. Local lifestyles inspired its next product line, an automatic, one-gallon home milk pasteurizer. Many farm families were drinking raw milk, a dangerous practice that often caused undulant fever, a milk-transmitted disease. The company began designing its pasteurizer in 1946. One year later the product was introduced by Sears, Roebuck & Company under the Farm Master brand name.

But the company saw its real future in the manufacture and sale of electronic equipment for medical research. Working in conjunction with the aeromedical department of Mayo Clinic, the company designed a variety of medical instruments including a cardiotachometer for measurement of instantaneous heart rate, an oximeter for measurement of oxygen content in blood, and a nitrogen meter for measurement of lung functions. The Medical Equipment Division also designed an aseptic, automatic surgical camera which could be sterilized. This division was the forerunner of Waters Instruments, Inc.

When fighting erupted in Korea, Waters Conley again contributed to national defense, signing a $1,003,002 contract with the U.S. Signal Corps for 338 code practice equipment machines. Impressed with the company's diverse history, a *Rochester Post-Bulletin* reporter commented, "The old Waters-Conley plant in northwest Rochester has more lives than a cat." In 1960 Waters Conley was purchased by Telex Corporation. The product line was again changed, this time to hearing aids and headphones.

Along Highway 52 the glistening blue windows of International Business Machines have become a city landmark. IBM did not move to Rochester by accident. Selection of Rochester as a plant site occurred as a result of the combined efforts of Governor Orville Freeman's Committee of 100 and a group of local business leaders who banded together to form Industrial Opportunities, Incorporated (IOI). Governor Freeman's Committee of 100 actually consisted of more than 200 business, professional, labor, and civic leaders who worked in tandem to attract new businesses to Minnesota. Similarly, IOI explored new ways to entice businesses to Rochester.

To launch its $200,000 fund-raising campaign, IOI representatives fired a toy cannon on a downtown street corner. Two employees of IBM who happened to be in Rochester scouting the area as a possible plant site, "part of a quiet review of 80 cities of 25,000 to 75,000 population in several midwestern states," according to *25th Anniversary*, a special IBM publication, witnessed the ceremony. The IBM employees were impressed by the enthusiasm of local businessmen.

The publicity stunt also paid off. Several months later the *Rochester Post-Bulletin* ran the headline "IBM to Erect Huge Plant Here: 1,500 to be Employed by 1958." Temporary quarters for IBM employees were needed while the plant was under construction. Unable to find a suitable building, IBM enlisted the aid of IOI, which agreed to build the structure and lease it to the company for 10 years.

Harold Kamm had been selected man-

ager of IOI and was responsible for recruiting new businesses to Rochester. Under Kamm's leadership IOI raised funds for a 50,000-square-foot facility which would be built on a 140-acre site in northwest Rochester. Cost of the building was $480,000 and included a 250-car parking lot, sidewalks, and landscaped lawns. Construction of a road from Highway 52 west to the Chicago Great Western Railroad tracks was also part of the ambitious project.

"The excitement surrounding the firing of the tiny toy cannon on a downtown street corner had hit its mark: IBM and the city of Rochester were already growing together," reported *25th Anniversary.*

Kamm's life story proved to be a subplot in the IBM drama. Recognizing Kamm's energy and expertise, the company offered him the position of Coordinator of Unit Training, based in the IOI building. Kamm tendered his resignation to IOI and at age 36 launched a new career. IOI president Arthur Hirman expressed appreciation for the work Kamm had done for the Rochester community and wished him well in his new position.

Members of the Committee of 100 were eager to learn how Rochester had managed to attract IBM. In a report to Governor Freeman and the committee, Kamm said the city's esprit de corps had much to do with IOI's success. Hundreds of organizations had contributed to this success, explained Kamm, who expressed the hope that Rochester's good fortune would rub off on the rest of the state.

Not everyone was cheering Rochester, however. "Winona Is Envious," cried a headline in the February 13, 1956, issue of the *Post-Bulletin.* Reprinted from the *Winona Daily News,* the article congratulated Rochester and pondered its success. Assets of both cities were compared. "But Rochester got

the plum and we're happy for her," conceded the writer.

Albert Williams, executive vice president of IBM, in a speech to the Rochester Area Chamber of Commerce, explained IBM's reasons for selecting Rochester. "There are many things we take into consideration," noted Williams, who listed availability of manpower, transportation facilities, quality of education, and medical facilities as some of the main reasons. Williams acknowledged that other highly rated cities had been considered. "Why, then, did we select Rochester?" he asked. His answer warmed the cockles of media and midwestern hearts. "All in all we found no warmer, more intelligent community than Rochester."

IBM selected Eero Saarinen as its architect. Saarinen had designed the General Motors Technical Center in Warren, Michigan; the U.S. Embassy Office Building in London, England; and the Massachusetts Institute of Technology chapel in Cambridge, Massachusetts. He envisioned a spacious IBM campus, with modern buildings and open areas balancing each other. Groundbreaking for the facility began on July 31, 1956, when giant tractor blades scraped across the cornfields.

This land had originally belonged to early Rochester settlers George Dow, Ephraim Cobb, Perez Cobb, George Carpenter, and Taylor Carpenter. The Dubuque

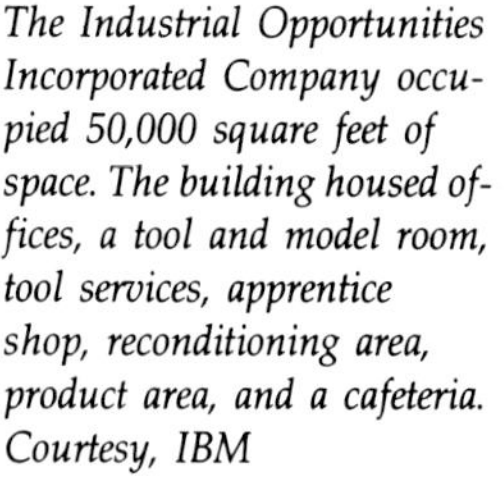

The Industrial Opportunities Incorporated Company occupied 50,000 square feet of space. The building housed offices, a tool and model room, tool services, apprentice shop, reconditioning area, product area, and a cafeteria. Courtesy, IBM

Trail crossed a portion of this land, and an old schoolhouse, built in 1860, stood where the entrance of the plant is now located.

The IBM facilities were built by the Minneapolis firm of Johnson, Drake and Piper, which wasted no time in getting started. Buildings seemed to burst from the ground like mushrooms. A 60,000-square-foot warehouse was constructed first, followed by the construction of the lobby in the main building, which took only six weeks. Simulating earlier history, a railroad spur line was laid to connect IBM with the Mankato and Osage, Iowa, lines.

Charles J. Lawson, Jr., was appointed general manager of IBM. He supervised five division managers: personnel, engineering, purchasing, manufacturing, and controller. Most employees, 121 out of a total of 174, were from the Rochester area. "About 20 per cent of the total IBM work force here will be of a professional status, development engineers, administrators, etc." reported a February 8, 1956, *Post-Bulletin* article.

Lawson surprised employees, city officials, and media representatives with an announcement at an October 5, 1956, luncheon meeting. Construction plans had been expanded. Another 150,000 square feet of space would be added to the plant, increasing total square footage by 37.5 percent. Work proceeded on schedule and dedication ceremonies were held on October 1, 1958.

More than 25,000 people attended the day-long celebration. Highway 52 became one massive traffic jam as cars, wedged bumper-to-bumper, slowed to enter the IBM campus. Traffic slowed somewhat in the afternoon when it began to rain. Governor Freeman, Philip Pillsbury, and Dr. Charles Mayo were among the many dignitaries who witnessed the lowering of a time capsule into the ground.

Contents of the capsule included an American flag, federal and state tax forms, a dictionary, a company benefits packet, a pair of safety glasses, a copy of the IBM song entitled "Ever Onward," a history of IBM, and copies of the Olmsted County Historical Society newsletter. Later a metal plate was placed over the capsule to mark its location. On September 20, 2058, the capsule is scheduled to be reopened.

Components for punch-card collators were transported from Endicott, New York, to Rochester by the Flying Tiger Freight Line. The Flying Tigers achieved fame during World War II under the leadership of Major General Claire Chennault. A photograph in the September 22, 1956, edition of the *Rochester Post-Bulletin* showed John David, manager of warehousing, accepting parts from copilot La Mont Shadowens.

Northwest Airlines celebrated its 30th anniversary on October 12, 1956, with the landing of a Ford Tri Motor in Rochester. The plane had a cruising speed of 100 m.p.h. Courtesy, Olmsted County Historical Society Society

IBM adopted an eight-bar logo in 1970. Here a worker installs a new identification with the logo on it near Highway 52. Courtesy, IBM

The IBM Type 552 Alphabetical Interpreter was first to roll off the assembly line. By August 1957 the Rochester plant had another nine products in production: 077 NumericCollator, 089 Alphabetic Collator, 514 Reproducing Punch, 519 Document Originating Machine, 521 Electronic Calculating Punch-Computing Punch Unit, 523 Gang Summary Punch, 533 Read Punch Unit, 549 Ticket Converter, and the 323 (an input/output source for the RAMAC system). "Made in Rochester" was no longer a dream. It had become reality.

Safety became a top priority. Engineer Robert McCutcheon was appointed IBM's head of safety. McCutcheon explained the company's safety procedures to a *Post-Bulletin* reporter on February 21, 1957. "In order to do this [prevent accidents] all machines are inspected to guard against any potential pinch points, open gears, V-belts and electric pulleys," McCutcheon said.

IBM's long-term commitment to safety was recognized. In 1967 the Rochester plant received a national award of honor for having the safest plant of its kind in the nation (based upon the last quarter of the year). "The award was a result of the plant's record 5,809,762 man-hours worked without a disabling injury," noted *25th Anniversary.*

In June 1961 the IBM Development Laboratory opened, expanding the company's product line. Additional product support was supplied by the Product Testing Laboratory, which opened in November 1961. According to *25th Anniversary,* "With the installation of the chamber, IBM Rochester products could now be tested in the same severe environmental conditions that the products could face in their worldwide use." But IBM didn't just care about products, it cared about people.

Employee services were expanded to meet the needs of a growing work force. The Speak Up! program was launched in 1962 and gave employees a way to air complaints and opinions. Later the scope of the program was broadened to include queries and informational requests. IBMers were also given direct access to qualified personnel, rather than waiting for written communication from them.

Employees reveled in the first Family Day Picnic, held at Silver Lake Park on Sep-

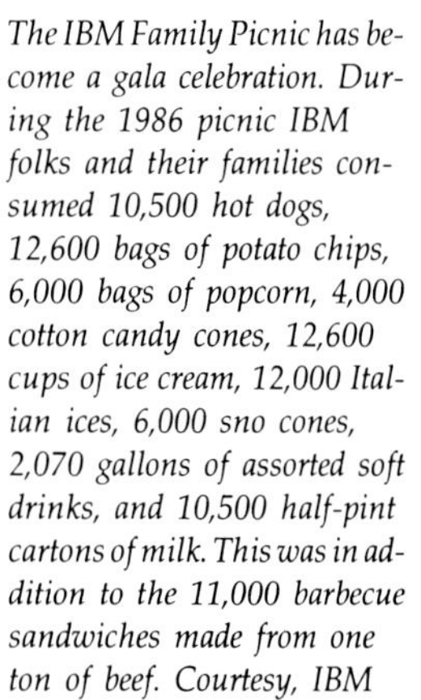

The IBM Family Picnic has become a gala celebration. During the 1986 picnic IBM folks and their families consumed 10,500 hot dogs, 12,600 bags of potato chips, 6,000 bags of popcorn, 4,000 cotton candy cones, 12,600 cups of ice cream, 12,000 Italian ices, 6,000 sno cones, 2,070 gallons of assorted soft drinks, and 10,500 half-pint cartons of milk. This was in addition to the 11,000 barbecue sandwiches made from one ton of beef. Courtesy, IBM

tember 22, 1956. Children could hardly choose from among the pony rides, picnic food, and games. In time this annual picnic drew crowds so large that IBM moved the event to a five-acre park bordering Highway 52. The IBM Club even sponsored a contest to name the park. Woodside Park was the winning entry. Respecting history, IBM preserved the huge red barn which stood on the site.

The Family Day Picnic became a festive event featuring a carnival and nationally known entertainers such as the Osmond Brothers. Carnival workers converged on the grasslands adjoining the plant and magically (or so it seemed) set up rides within 48 hours. Local students were hired to help operate the rides. IBMers and their families enjoyed standard picnic fare—barbecues, hot dogs, potato chips, milk, coffee, and pop— served free of charge.

IBM also offered to their employees educational opportunities, which ranged from technical courses to management training. During 1987 the IBM Education Department logged between 35,000 to 40,000 student days of education. In some instances professors were hired to come on-site to teach IBM employees.

September 30, 1973, was a historic date for both IBM and Mayo Clinic. On this day Mayo Clinic and St. Marys Hospital were linked together by computer. "Bedside instrumentation jointly developed by IBM and Mayo Clinic went into use for the first time at the opening of Saint Marys' new 12-bed Cardiac Post-Operative Recovery Unit," reported *25th Anniversary*. With the acquisition of hospitals and the opening of satellite clinics, Mayo Clinic's use of computers increased markedly.

It is impossible to catalog Mayo Clinic inventions here; they would be a book by themselves. Since the days when Dr. Charlie invented his own operating table, Mayo Clinic physicians have continued to invent surgical tools, procedures, and equipment. The photoelectric colorimeter, invented by Dr. Arthur H. Sanford, exemplifies Mayo's contributions to technology. Dr. Sanford's in-vention, which measured the quantitative determination of hemoglobin, became the primary method of quantifying chemicals in body fluids.

Dr. Sanford described his photoelectric colorimeter in 1929. The first commercial model was manufactured in 1932. One year later Dr. Sanford received the Ward Burdick gold medal from the American Society of Clinical Pathologists in recognition of his achievement. He also received the Distinguished Service Award from Northwestern University in 1940 and the American Pathologists' Scientific Products Foundation Award in 1956.

Mayo Clinic was the first medical institution in the nation to install an Emiscanner. Manufactured by Electronic Music, Incorporated (EMI), which made instruments for the musical group, The Beatles, this high-tech device revolutionized diagnostics. The Emiscanner was 100 times more sensitive than normal X rays and, unlike previous procedures that injected air and dye into the brain, this technique was harmless to patients. Patient mortality dropped to zero. Moreover, the Emiscanner required only the services of a single trained radiographer, freeing up other medical personnel.

From a prone position the patient placed his head halfway inside the scanner. Once activated, the scanner's tube moved across the top of the head while the scanner revolved around the head in 180 one-degree increments. Test results were available within 15 minutes. Computerized data was produced in the form of photographs or numerical printouts. Emiscanner quickly became known as computerized axial tomography. This name was shortened to computerized tomography, or CT scan, as it is called today.

The imaginations of Rochester inventors seem boundless. It is impossible to predict what technological advances the future will hold. Together, the combined technological achievements of Mayo Clinic and IBM literally span the globe—a far cry from the knuckle joint oscillating bob sleigh.

The Colonial and Allied
Hospitals School of Nursing
opened in 1918. In 1954 the
name of the school was
changed to the Methodist-
Kahler School of Nursing.
Courtesy, Methodist
Hospital

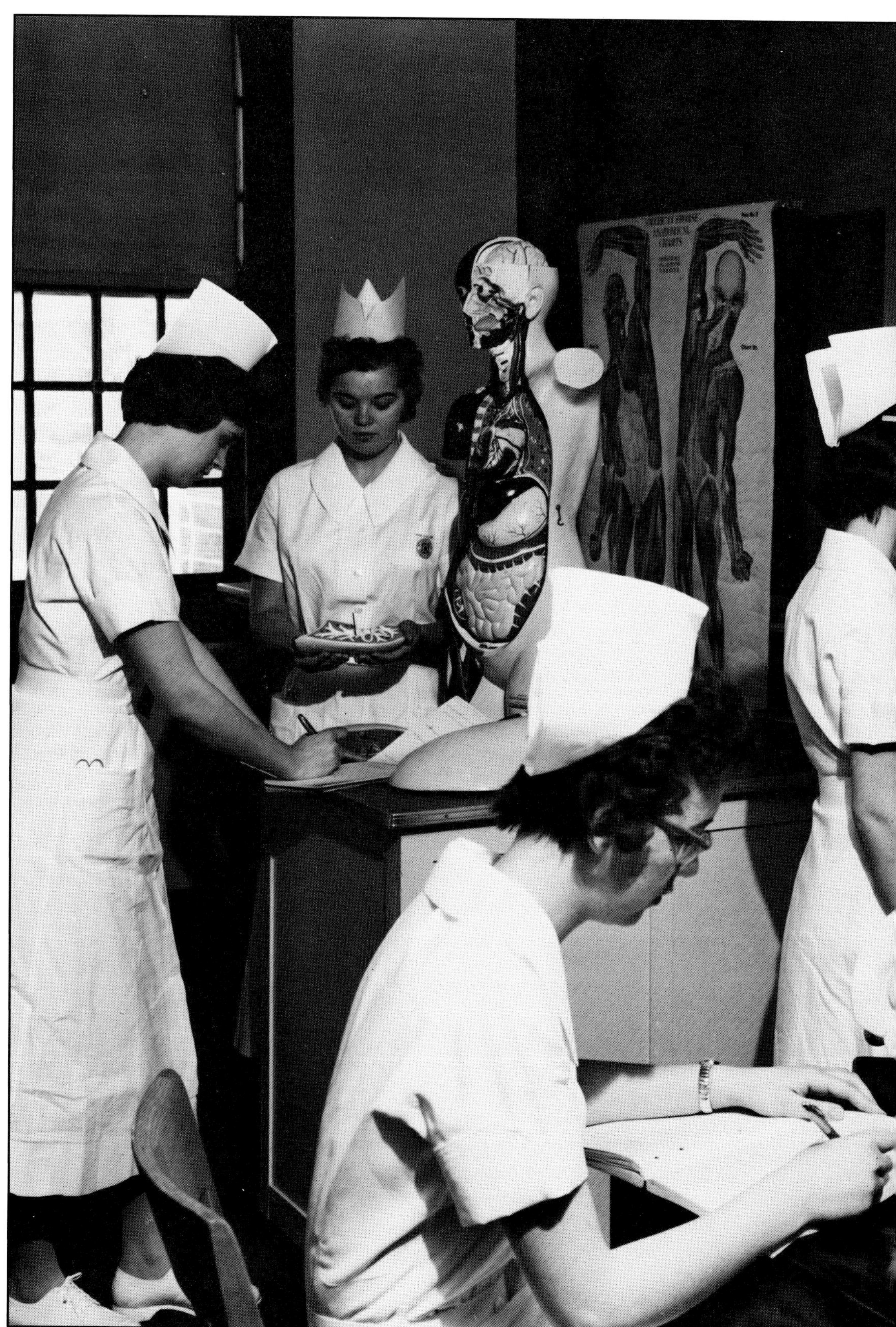

5

MORE THAN MCGUFFEY READERS

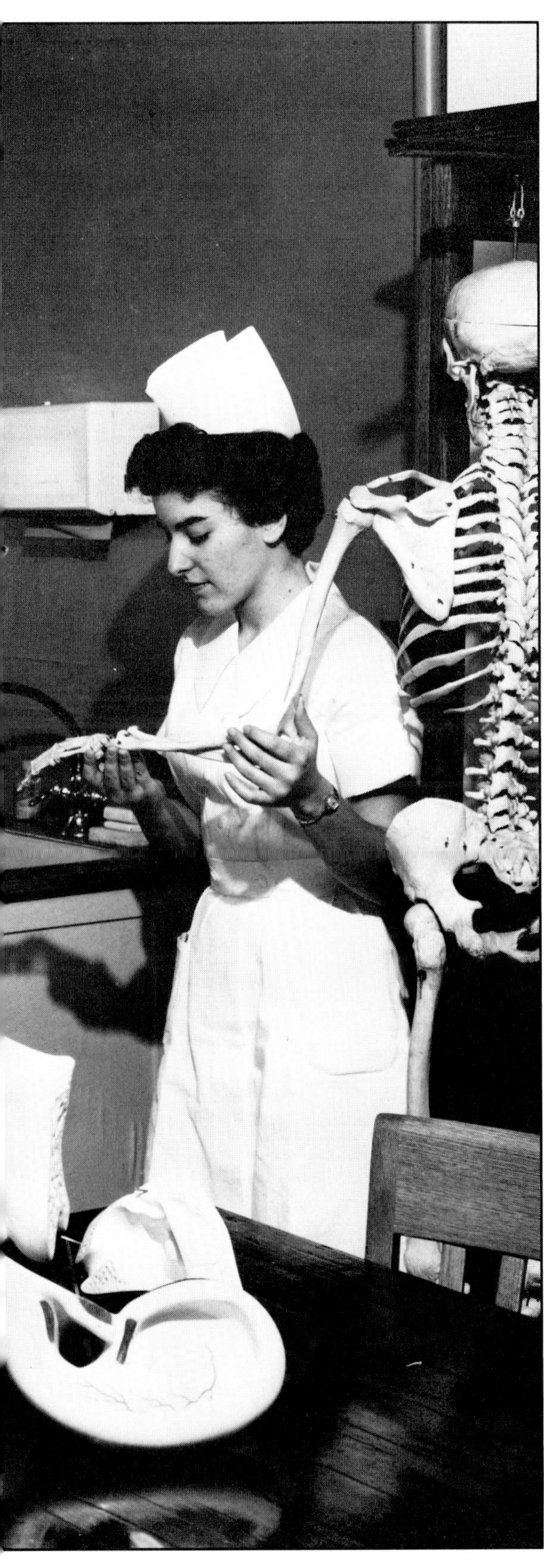

Sanford Niles was the hero of Rochester education, yet few remember his name or accomplishments. History offered Niles, Olmsted County's first superintendent of schools, the opportunity to shape education. He grabbed it. Niles established training programs for teachers, wrote a comprehensive curriculum for students, and worked tirelessly to upgrade schools and equipment. "Rochester should remember that her school buildings and public schools are her chief glory today," commented Niles in 1883.

The Organic Act of the Territory of Minnesota provided the basis for education in the state. Effective March 3, 1849, this farsighted legislation detailed tax mill rates and procedures for acquiring school properties. By 1858 there were 49 schoolhouses scattered throughout Olmsted County.

These first schoolhouses were a community effort. The raising of a schoolhouse was an exciting, festive community event. Materials and labor were usually donated. Volunteers erected the walls first, followed by framing of windows and doors. Crude benches and a master's desk, "fearfully and wonderfully made," as Niles put it, were built last. Yet some volunteer workmanship was substandard, as an 1866 entry in Niles' school diary attests, "Log house, poorly chinked, poor seats, and without blackboards."

Niles, an indefatigable supervisor, believed in on-site inspections. During his 11 years as superintendent, Niles traversed Olmsted County 22 times, making 2,600 official school visits. Recalled Niles' daughter Mabel, "He said he could visit a school while he was caring for his horse." Of the county's 77 schoolhouses Niles visited in 1865, he was horrified to discover that 56 had no outhouses and 11 no blackboards.

The first schools in Olmsted County had little equipment. In 1866 Sanford Niles determined that basic equipment would include a water pail, dipper, wash basin, and towel. Later Niles added a blackboard, crayons, numerical frame globe, cube root blocks, a United States map, and a copy of Webster's Dictionary. *Courtesy, Olmsted County Historical Society*

The Sanford Niles family portrait of 1900 shows Niles with his wife, Priscilla, son Oliver, and daughter Mabel. Following his death on July 8, 1905, an unnamed state education newspaper paid tribute to Niles. "The kindly man always controlled him," said the obituary. Courtesy, Olmsted County Historical Society

Teaching records were often sketchy or nonexistent. "The names of early teachers were not a matter of record," lamented Niles, "and they were seldom preserved." According to private testimony Susan Rucker, Rochester's first teacher, taught in a log schoolhouse during the winter of 1855-1856. And city clerk records for 1857 list only Phebe Hoag and Miss Stedman as teachers.

Niles, though, became one of the most famous men in Olmsted County, a reputa-

tion partly due to his adjunct career as an author. Niles wrote *A Teacher's Guide and Course of Study for District Schools,* the first such curriculum in the state. He also wrote a weekly education column for the *Rochester Post.* Niles' textbooks, *A Geography of Minnesota, History of the United States, History and Government of Minnesota,* and *Niles' Advanced Geography: Mathematical, Physical, Political,* were used in schools throughout the nation. Naturally, Niles' educational philosophy was expressed in his writing.

Niles' educational philosophy was enlightened for his time. He considered the pupil to be a constant observer. Students were encouraged to be self-reliant, creative thinkers. Teachers were urged not to rely on rote lessons but to adopt a topical, or thematic, approach. Reading should be taught in an "easy, natural manner," said Niles, similar to daily conversation.

Because children were needed at home to plant, tend, and harvest crops, school was in session only four months a year. Seasonal variables also affected attendance. Explained Niles, "When potatobugs are plentiful, when large fields of corn are planted, or the school term ex-

tends past the time for haying, pupils will be kept out to pick berries, to gather bugs, to plant and weed corn, to assist in haying."

During 1861 there were 133 people between the ages of 5 and 21 living in Olmsted County. Out of this total, 50 attended school for three months. School attendance figures peaked in 1877 but declined sharply in 1883 because of "Western fever" and the growth of private schools.

Teaching, whether in a private or public school, was regarded as last-resort employment. "Even ordinary trades offer better inducements," conceded Niles. Female teachers received significantly lower salaries than their male counterparts. Records for 1862 list wages for male teachers at $16.75 a month, contrasted to $12 a month for female teachers. Salary discrepancies, even cuts, were accepted by the public. "The average monthly compensation of female teachers has been somewhat reduced as the number [of female teachers] has increased," Niles reported in *History of Olmsted County, Minnesota.*

In 1881 the state legislature ordered publication of *Laws of Minnesota Relating to the Public Schools and the State Normal Schools.* These laws granted women age 21 or older the right to sign petitions and vote at school meetings. However, ballots cast by female voters had to be deposited in a separate box. The document also divided public schools into common, independent, and special districts.

Rochester's first public school students learned to read from used, worn texts purchased from other states. Minnesota made a concerted effort to standardize materials and in 1858 passed a mandate authorizing superintendents to introduce and recommend suitable textbooks. "Under this law," reported Niles, "Robinson's arithmetics, Parker and Watson's readers, Monteith's and McNally's geographies and Goodrich's history came into general use in the county." Today's school workbooks and computer programs still use many of the same teach-

ing exercises found in the old textbooks: fill in the blanks, find likenesses and differences, and creative writing.

Niles was also concerned about the ability and training of area teachers. Unprepared and frightened, a stunning 33⅓ percent of Olmsted County teachers resigned annually. (Many female teachers were forced to resign when they married.) "How can the largest number of trained teachers be secured for county schools?" Niles asked. His solution was a teacher-training program. In 1865 Niles in-

McGuffey's Eclectic Spelling Book, published in 1879, contained drawings of prairie objects easily recognized by young children. These texts became standard resources in the Midwest. By 1925 a total of 122 million McGuffey readers had been sold nationally. Courtesy, Olmsted County Historical Society

PICTORIAL ALPHABET.

A **a**	Ax	**B** **b**	Boy
C **c**	Cat	**D** **d**	Dog
E **e**	Elk	**F** **f**	Fox
G **g**	Girl	**H** **h**	Hen

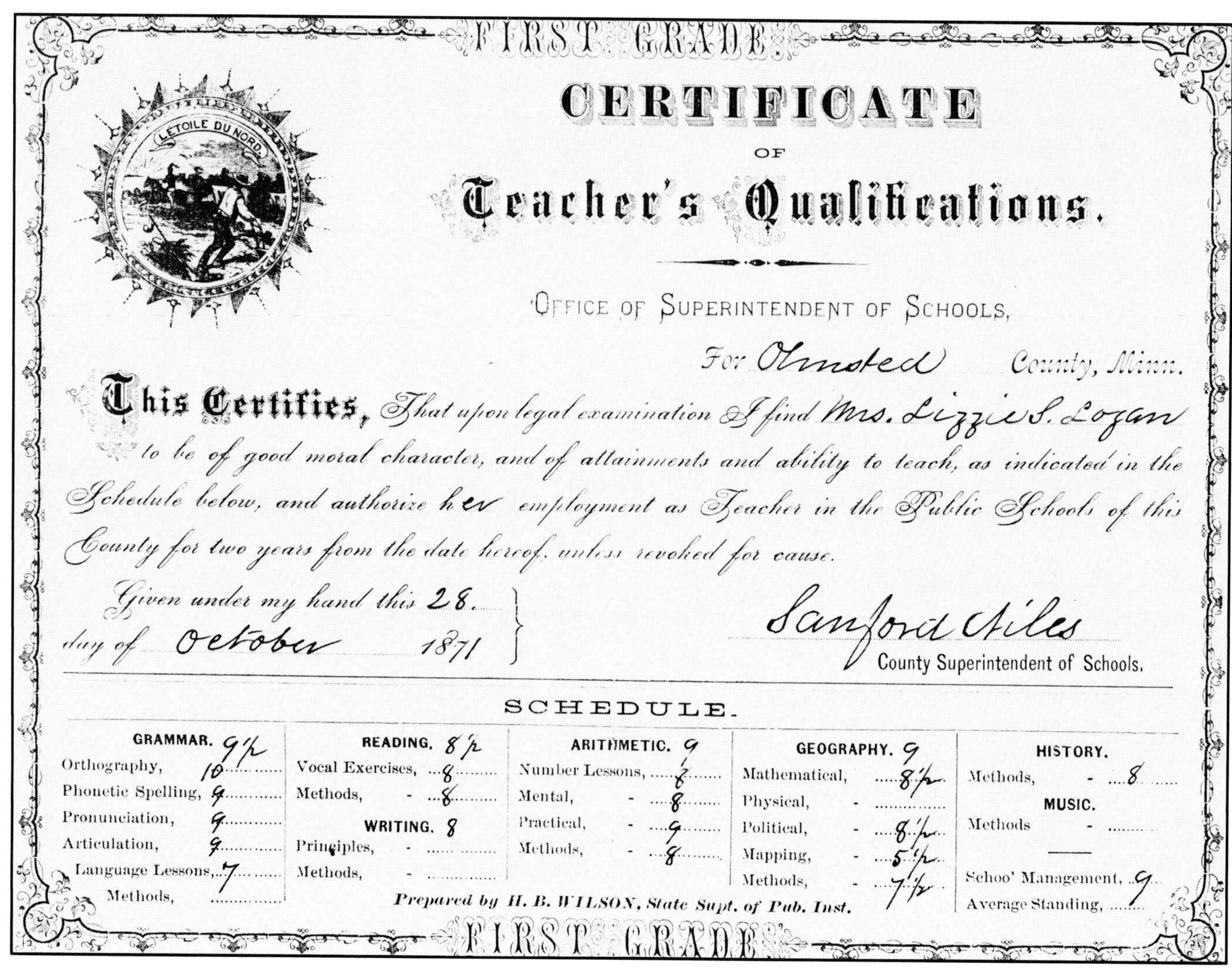

The signature of Sanford Niles is evident on this first grade teaching certificate, issued to Lizzie Logan. In order to receive her certificate, Logan had to pass a variety of exams. Presumably, 10 was the highest score a teaching candidate could receive. Logan's scores are high, with the exception of her score in mapping, kindly overlooked by geographer Niles. Courtesy, Olmsted County Historical Society

itiated the first Teachers' Training Institute. Twenty-five such institutes were held during his tenure.

"These training schools have become established features of the education system of this county, and their advantages are so thoroughly known that they need no commendation," reported the *Rochester Post* on March 22, 1873. The fee for the institute was two dollars. Teachers were divided into two groups according to ability: the first group was composed of teachers with "considerable scholarship and experience" and the second of beginners with "more limited attainments."

Teachers were evaluated by examination. Uniform County Teachers' Examinations were given to every teaching candi-

date prior to employment. Exams covered reading, writing, geography, grammar, spelling, hygiene, math, United States history, and civics. Yet teachers who were awarded these certificates were not "home free." Space was provided on the certificates for follow-up notes by school officials who would comment on classroom control, organization, and teaching methods.

Construction of Central School in 1868 exemplified, in brick and mortar, Rochester's commitment to education. There are conflicting reports about the cost of construction, but it is believed to have been $75,000. "It is an investment which pays, and our central building may stand to honor its projectors when every child now within its walls had ceased to walk the earth," wrote Niles in *History of Olmsted County, Minnesota.*

Newspaper accounts referred to the building's "extreme" height and dimensions. *Rochester Post* readers were dazzled by numbers: 112 windows, 300 cords of stone, 70,000 bricks, 14 rooms, and 2 towers. The south tower housed an observatory and the north tower housed a bell. The bell, specially cast at the Menceley Bell Foundry in Troy, New York, was proudly inscribed, "Public School of the City of Rochester, A.D. 1868."

William Hein—Heinie to his friends—worked as a janitor at Central School for 40 years. Among Heinie's many jobs was ringing the bell. He "wakened Rochester, sent it to school and to work, and tolled the end of its day," wrote the author of "Heinie, the Bell Ringer of Central School." Heinie was also responsible for the flag system which was used to "broadcast" weather reports to Rochester residents. A white flag signaled clear weather, a white flag topped by blue signaled fair and warmer, a white flag supported by blue signaled fair and colder, and a blue flag signaled an impending storm.

On September 1, 1910, fire broke out, destroying the top two floors and both towers of Central School. "Flames licked furiously upward and smoke belched out in clouds. In the center of the inferno the old bell swung back and forth, tolling its own funeral," continued the author of "Heinie." The heat was so intense it began to melt and distort the bell. When water from fire hoses hit the hot metal, the 1,500-pound bell plunged through four floors into the basement and shattered into pieces. Central School, however, was reroofed and served as a grade school until the new Central opened in 1926.

In 1921 approximately 700 graduates of Central School assembled for a reunion of the Old Boys and Old Girls clubs. The reunion had originally been organized five years earlier as the Old Boys Club but alumnae demanded equal representation. Dr. Will and Dr. Charlie spoke at the evening banquet, along with John Willis Bear of Los Angeles. The *Daily Post and Record,* on October 8, 1921, quoted Bear as saying, "You can't keep us away. We have come to dedicate ourselves anew."

Spelling bees were an important annual event, a blend of spelling drill and cheap community entertainment. The May 8, 1875, edition of *Recipes Abroad for Folks at Home* was the prize for older contestants and *Picture Book of the Sagacity of Animals* was the prize for younger contestants. "They are both of them beautiful books," observed a reporter, "full of handsome pictures, that would delight the heart of any child."

Central School, completed in 1868, was for many years the tallest building in Rochester. Courtesy, Olmsted County Historical Society

Historians believe this class portrait was taken outside Phelps School. Its wood frame construction and lack of fire escapes caused the school to be condemned in 1915. Courtesy, Olmsted County Historical Society

Spelling bees survived for decades, even if rural teachers did not. F.L. Cook, education editor of the *Rochester Post*, reported on April 4, 1884, that complaints about rural teachers had been received. "Many of the superintendents and teachers of the state are watching our school work in the county with great interest. Some of them say, that, taken as a class, the teachers in the country schools do not know enough to use a course of study."

Cook thought the accusation unfounded. "Our progress has been very satisfactory and the outlook is extremely flattering," replied the editor. His comment was followed by two notices demonstrating his point: the state institute coordinator would be visiting local schools and results of teachers' exams would be disclosed within a month.

Yet two weeks later Cook himself complained about education, specifically, poor punctuation. Students were trained to write script, admitted Cook, but they were not sufficiently trained in punctuation. Cook, who considered punctuation an "easy and interesting subject," then printed part of a chapter from *Bardeen's Rhetoric* and directed readers to save the excerpt for future reference.

A host of private schools opened in Rochester and many were aimed at female students. Rochester Academy opened in 1861; its curriculum included painting, music, and drawing. In 1863 Rochester Seminary for Young Ladies opened, offering courses in English, French, German, music, drawing, needlework, and waxwork. Rochester Female Institute, established in 1864, included in its curriculum "solid and ornamental" branches of learning, according to Niles.

In 1877 the Academy of Our Lady of Lourdes was established. Mother Alfred had been sent to Rochester to organize the academy, which served as a motherhouse for the Sisters of Saint Francis. Enrollment rose rapidly and in 1882 the sisters purchased a larger building. But the 1888 addition proved to be only a stopgap measure. Two more parochial schools were built in 1912: Heffron High School for boys and St. John's for girls. Both schools functioned well until the Christian Brothers, who taught at Heffron, moved from Rochester in 1925. Necessity forced the two schools to merge into what was the forerunner of today's Lourdes High School.

In 1865 the Rochester Seminary opened and was the first school to offer high school courses. Discipline was emphasized and utmost care was taken to promote the moral development of students, "bringing them to act under the salutary influence of religion principles." The school incorporated in 1883 and finally built a $12,000 brick building which could accommodate 300 students.

Some of the oldest documents on file at the Olmsted County Historical Society are early copies of *The Rochester Seminary*

*These graduates of Darling'
Business College, circa 1905,
are ready to tackle the
future. Courtesy, Olmsted
County Historical Society*

Gazette. The fall 1865 issue contained articles about happiness, sympathy, sunshine, and politeness. "The heart always warms toward one, whom the world calls grateful and kind," said the writer.

The public seemed neither grateful nor kind when Niles was ousted in 1876 and M.G. Spring was elected superintendent of schools. Yet Niles' commitment to education never faltered. He and his wife, Priscilla, opened the Rochester English and Classical School. Priscilla Niles was a unique woman, a true partner. Her first teaching job was in a Vermont school system where she earned two dollars a week, the same salary she had made working in a Lowell, Massachusetts, mill.

Rochester English and Classical School had three terms: fall, winter, and spring. Courses covered English, Latin, Greek, French, German, and bookkeeping. Supplementary fees were charged for language training. English cost an additional seven dollars per term, French and German cost an additional four dollars per term, and Latin and Greek cost an additional three dollars. In 1885 Niles purchased *School Education* magazine and the couple moved to Minneapolis.

Special training and business schools were also established. Darling's Business College, established in 1879, had two major departments, preparatory and commercial. This specialized school obviously met a local need because its student body in-

creased rapidly, as did its curriculum. The *Rochester Post* of January 16, 1880, said the school offered a good, sound, and practical business education, which was "an inheritance that fadeth not away."

Furthermore, said the newspaper, Rochester was blessed to have such a school. The newspaper sent a reporter to observe Darling's Business College in action. When he returned the reporter said the school's site was convenient and its rooms were well lighted and well furnished. What impressed the reporter most was the mock-up of an actual business department, with the bond broker's desk, bankers' desks, and skits of "actual monied transactions" using fake currency.

These schools emphasized penmanship as well as artwork which could be executed using penmanship techniques. The *Rochester Post* of October 9, 1891, praised Professor Holt's exhibition at the fairgrounds. Holt was a penmanship teacher at Darling's Business College. President Zaner, of the Zanerian Art College in Columbus, Ohio, visited the exhibition and was struck by Holt's work. "If his [Holt's] equal exists I do not know it," said Zaner.

Trade schools also were formed. In 1896 the Rochester Industrial School was founded. Students could choose from among a shorthand and typing curriculum, preparatory course, teachers training course, or commercial course. The Roch-

At one time the Rochester Public Library was located at city hall. In 1937 a library facility was built at the cost of $178,000. H.H. Crawford designed the Minnesota dolomite limestone building, which featured an owl above the front entry. Courtesy, Olmsted County Historical Society

ester Business College and School of Telegraphy opened on East Zumbro Street with a huge advertisement in the *Olmsted County Democrat* detailing the growing need for trained business workers: "This is the only college in the land that is capable of teaching you a thorough business course in Rapid Calculation." Telegraphy training was offered to both men and women, who were told their training would lead to good positions afterward.

The Rochester Business and Normal College was a bit more modest in its promotion. While the college catalog did not guarantee positions, it said the school would use its best endeavors to secure positions for students. "It is a business college in the full sense of the word," said the school catalog. The catalog also highlighted the school's emphasis on spelling. "The manner in which Spelling is slighted in nearly all our schools and the great number of poor spellers resulting therefrom is really astounding, and emphasize the crying need of more work in this much neglected subject," stated the catalog. As a remedy, Rochester Business and Normal College students were obligated to spend part of each day on spelling.

The school's 1905 program contained the class motto, "To Be, Not to Seem," and the class yell, a nonsensical tongue twister. Anyone who could say it, let alone yell it, deserved employment:

Whangeroozle—Tapulacobuse—
Rip—Snorter—Junk!
Bookkeepers—Typewriters—
We never flunk!
Rooshawhacker—Woolipaloozer—
Ghouls—Ghosts—Banchee!
Normalites—Shorthand—Sprites—
R.B. & N.C.

Educational opportunities were not confined to formal schools. Mr. Sykes organized a fencing class for 16 inmates at the Rochester State Hospital. Miss Robin advertised her French and German classes in *The Rochester Post.* And at Darling's Business College, Amanda Kidder opened a school for the Art of Expression and Physical Culture.

Twelve years after Rochester was founded, the city was still without a library. (Although Niles maintained a teaching library in his home—one of the first such libraries in the state—this service was not a substitute for a public library.) Some concerned citizens met in 1866 to organize a public library system. John D. Blake was elected president of the Library Association and Lewis Walker was elected secretary. Walker also served as librarian. Public donations financed the initial purchase of 1,000 volumes.

Dr. W.W. Mayo agreed to serve on the library board. His influence was substantial, according to biographer Helen Clapesattle. "He took the initiative in establishing a city library and stocking it with books," she wrote. Dr. Will helped to plan an annual lecture series, luring such famous speakers to Rochester as Horace Greeley, founder and editor of the *New York Tribune* and candidate for the U.S. presidency in 1872.

Many of the books on the library's shelves were classics. *Catalog of the Rochester Library,* published in 1881, lists among its volumes *Aesop's Fables, Child's History* of England, by Charles Dickens, *Nicholas Nickleby,* also by Dickens, and *Familiar Quotations* by Bartlett. Despite this inventory, public interest in the library lagged. The Woman's Christian Temperance Union took charge of the library in 1883 and renamed it the Free Library and Reading Room Association. After a state statute provided for the organization of public libraries, Rochester lawyer Burt Eaton reorganized the Library Association. Eaton served as president until he was elected mayor of Rochester.

Performances by local amateur talent became fund-raising events for the library. A surprising amount of newspaper space was devoted to these productions. A May 8, 1875, article in the *Rochester Post* described two dramas, *Tenting Tonight* and *Woodcock's Little Game,* detailing the plots, dramatic techniques—such as voices singing offstage—and leading players. "It was very prettily done," observed the reporter, a comment which could be read as damning with faint praise.

Special libraries catering to Rochester's ethnic population were also established. The German Library Association was formed in the fall of 1866. Fourteen members attended the association's first meeting at the Minnesota House. The library was located in two cramped rooms above Vedder's warehouse. As the library grew it moved to a second location and eventually into Library Hall. Newspapers of the day often reported on the association's theater group and annual masked ball.

The Scandinavian Library Association was established in 1880. According to an April 2, 1880, article in the *Rochester Post,* the library had 250 volumes and was located on Bennett's block in Good Templar Hall. Meetings were held every Wednesday evening, "for literary and musical culture, a debate on some interesting topic held every fourth evening." In 1888 the Norwegian Library Association was organized. The group leased rooms on the third floor of a building on Horton's block and spruced up dingy walls with new wallpaper.

A MESSAGE FOR THE PEOPLE

IN REGARD TO

Rochester Chautauqua Assembly

= AND =

Harvest Home Festival

——•▶TO BE HELD IN◀•——

ROCHESTER, MINNESOTA

——FROM——

July 26th to August 2nd, 1907

S. T. NEVELN, Manager,
Iowa Chautauqua Builders' Association

8—GREAT DAYS—8
16—COMPLETE PROGRAMS—16
30—Special Entertainments—30

Season Tickets: - - Family, $5; Adult, $2; Child's, $1
Adult Single Admission: - - 50 cts., 35 cts. and 25 cts.
Child's Single Admission, - - - 25 cts., 20 cts., 15 cts.

Come and Bring Your Neighbors!

The Chautauqua movement, named after a lake in New York, began in 1874 as a course for Sunday school teachers. Cofounders John H. Vincent and Lewis Miller were leaders in the Methodist Chautauqua Camp Meeting Association, which offered a combination of education and recreation programs. By 1886 there were 50 branches in the nation. These traveling Chautauqua programs crisscrossed the country, hosting lectures, concerts, and recreational activities.

A Rochester Chautauqua Assembly program, dated 1907, billed entertainment as a lecture by Sir Walter Raleigh, a ladies quartet (singing Schubert), a magician, a male quartet, a moving picture company, and a Canadian band. "It is not only a Band but a Male Chorus of great ability," stated the program. "The drum major is 7 feet one and a half inches tall."

This 1907 Rochester Chautauqua Assembly program contained a list of 25 features. "Every feature worthy of approval by Rochester's best citizens." Courtesy, Olmsted County Historical Society

An outgrowth of the Chautauqua Assemblies was the establishment of local reading and study clubs, such as the Woman's Monday Club. Returning from a trip East, Mrs. C.H. Chandbourn founded the club in 1882. The club changed its name to the Senior History Class and finally settled on the name The Monday Club. "We Study for Light to Bless with Light" was the club's motto. Women were asked "never to bring into this study hour the problems of the day in church, home or civic life, but to devote the entire period to study," noted Lucy Stewart Herrick.

Herrick, a Central School teacher, preserved the club's history in a handwritten pamphlet. Study was so intense, she recalled, that there was no break for refreshments. Some pitying soul finally served coffee and doughnuts, a momentous event recorded in the club's archives with the comment, "It tasted mighty good." Upon completion of four years of study, much like high school, members received diplomas at a graduation ceremony. "All of the original 12 ladies were there and a merry time they had—it was an occasion they never tired talking about," wrote Herrick.

In 1892 The Study Club was founded. Alice Stinchfield Anderson, daughter of early Mayo partner Dr. Augustus Stinch-field, remembered "at the mid-point, after the paper was half given, why we had tea and little sandwiches or cookies or something." It is easy to confuse The Study Club with The Woman's Monday Club. Both clubs had the same purpose, both met on Mondays, both met for three hours, and to further baffle historians, two club members had the same last name, Eaton.

Why separate study clubs were formed is unclear. Perhaps the reasons were geographic, focus of study, or differences of opinion. For example, a taped history of The Study Club told about one member who resigned when a new member joined, because the new member's husband ran the local brewery. Whatever differences these clubs had, both filled an intellectual void in the lives of Rochester women.

Other study clubs were formed as well, including the Live and Learn Club and the Zumbro Valley Club. Like their predecessors, club members printed yearly programs listing topics of study.

But not all Rochester residents, it seemed, took an active part in studying or learning. George Howard, editor and publisher of the *Olmsted County Teacher*, wrote an article about Visiting Day in the February 1903 issue of the newsletter. Howard's article cited the lack of parental inter-

Left: Hoarfrost, the result of warm moist air coming into contact with colder tree limbs, turns Rochester into a winter fairyland. Photo by Gary Koenig

Below: Even geese don't want to get up on a sleepy, foggy morning. These geese huddle together on Silver Lake, warmed by the city power plant. Photo by Gary Koenig

With the onset of spring,
avid mushroom hunters are
out searching woodlands for
the elusive morels. Photo by
Gary Koenig

The St. Marys Park water tower in southwest Rochester has become a Rochester landmark. Photo by Gary Koenig

Artwork is scattered through-
out interiors and exteriors of
Mayo Foundation buildings.
The outstretched arms of
Ivan Mestrovic's sculpture
Man and Freedom *(on the
north wall of the Mayo Build-
ing) welcomes employees and
patients alike. Photo by
Gary Koenig*

St. Marys Hospital, part of the Mayo Foundation, serves patients from around the world. Photo by Gary Koenig

Left: These children, whizzing down the slide, epitomize fall fun in Rochester. Photo by Gary Koenig

Facing page, bottom: This stone bridge, built in the 1930s and partly funded by the Works Progress Administration, adds charm to Silver Lake Park. Photo by Gary Koenig

Left: At Silver Lake Park geese search for bread crumbs and corn kernels amidst the yellow leaves of autumn. Photo by Gary Koenig

The Mayo Medical School, formerly the public library, provides students with an ideal place to learn and study. Photo by Gary Koenig

est in students, curriculum, and materials. "How many of the parents or members of the board visit the school at all during the year?" he asked. Howard attempted to shame parents—through teachers—into visiting the schools. He wrote:

Not a man in Olmsted county would keep a valuable colt in training in an adjoining town, without making regular trips to town to see how the colt was progressing, and if the training wanted anything purchased for the colt's welfare it would be forthcoming immediately and no questions asked. Yet eight out of ten of these farmers will place their children, their priceless treasures, in training for 180 days in a year with one who is many times an entire stranger, and never spend one little minute going to see for themselves how the children are progressing . . .

With the establishment of St. Marys Hospital, there was a growing need for professional nursing training. Concerned with professional standards and licensure, Sister Joseph began a nursing school at St. Marys Hospital. At first the Doctors Mayo were against the idea. But Sister Joseph had faith in lay students and the influence of good management. She appointed a brilliant nurse, Anna Jammé, a graduate of the Johns Hopkins Training School for Nursing, as superintendent. Jammé accepted the challenge and the school opened in 1906 with two students.

Jammé thought students, too, faced a challenge: "To develop from a young, enthusiastic schoolgirl, [into] a woman, [into] a nurse who will fill an important place and take her part and leadership in the great scheme of woman's work of the future." Edith Graham Mayo, wife of Dr. Charlie, was the school's first nursing teacher. Students received 142 hours of instruction. Evaluation was based upon daily work, executive ability, compliance with rules, deportment, and ability to handle emergencies.

Following St. Marys' lead, the Colonial and Allied Hospitals School of Nursing

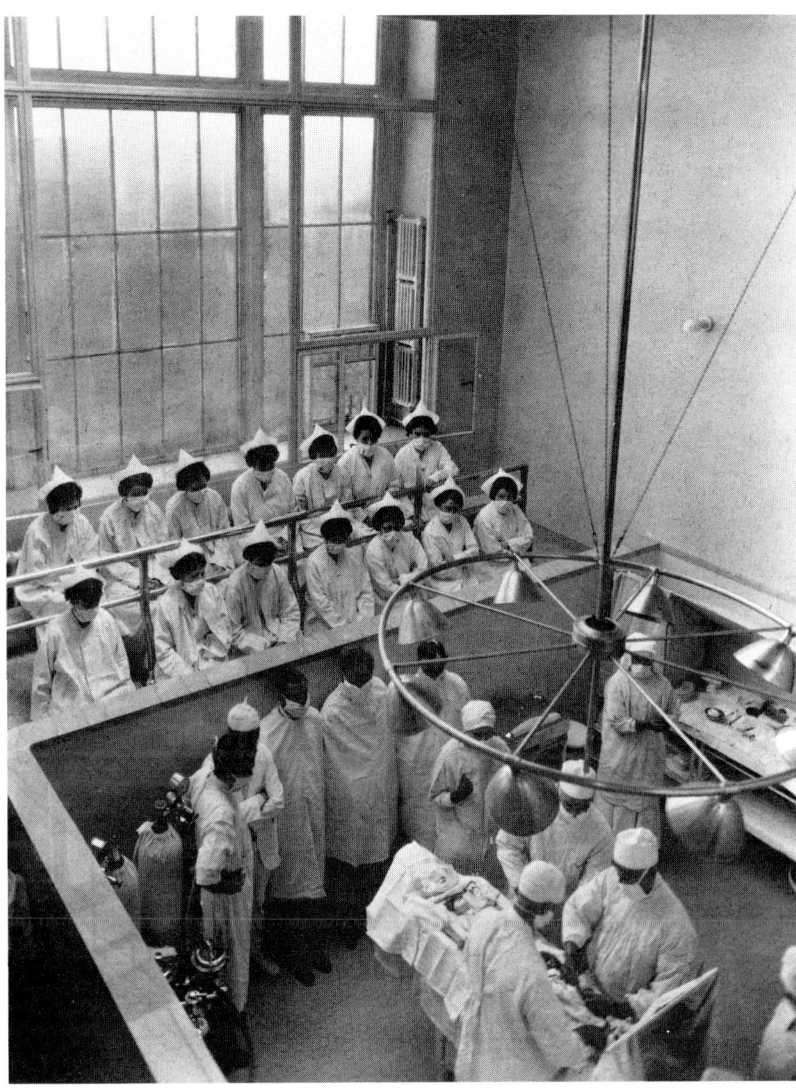

The St. Mary's School of Nursing students observe the famed Dr. Will in surgery. Courtesy, Olmsted County Historical Society

opened in 1918. According to the *Rochester Methodist Hospital News* of November 12, 1954, "the first students entered the school as part of a program to supply graduate nurses to civilian hospitals during W.W.I." Five students graduated from the initial one-year training program.

In 1922 the name of the school was changed to the Kahler Hospitals School of Nursing. In 1954 the name was changed again, to the Methodist-Kahler School of Nursing. Over the years, training requirements for nurses were expanded from two years of study to three, qualifying graduates for diplomas. Graduates of the school were placed in hospital positions across the nation and over-

The American Association of University Women sponsored Mary Martin's radio show, "Views and Interviews." The show used volunteer high school students as interviewers. C. John Hodgson and an unidentified student interviewed Eleanor Roosevelt when she visited Rochester in 1952. Mary Martin stands at the right. Courtesy, Dr. and Mrs. C. John Hodgson

posed adding an additional two years to high school training.

Most of RSJC's first students came from Rochester. By 1966, however, RSJC's student body was composed equally of Rochester residents and residents from surrounding communities. As the student body expanded, RSJC was forced to find additional classroom space, using facilities at the YWCA, at the armory, and at other public schools. Governor Karl Rolvaag pointed to RSJC as a pacesetter in the state. "If you had not kept it alive during the lean years I'm not sure we could today point with pride to the state system," said Rolvaag, speaking to members of Rochester civic clubs.

The Minnesota Bible College relocated in Rochester during 1971. Affiliated with the Church of Christ, the college was founded in Minneapolis in 1913. The college offered three degrees: Associate of Arts, Bachelor of Arts, and Bachelor of Science. Professor Eric Grice, a former dean of Minnesota Bible College, noted that Minnesota Bible College students were scattered throughout the world. "The 1950s saw students entering mission fields around the world including Japan, China, Tibet, India, the Philippines, South America and South Africa," said Grice in the November 5, 1987, edition of the *Rochester Post-Bulletin.*

In 1974 Independent School District 535 inaugurated its Community Education program, focusing on adult and continuing education. *Community Education: Comprehensive Plan* stated the mission of community education was to "offer a variety of lifelong learning experiences for the individual, family, and community of this school district." Moreover, the programs were not to focus on vocational training or academic degrees, but on self-learning.

Community Education welcomed course suggestions from the public. Everything from crafts to computer education was incorporated into the program. The spring/summer 1988 catalog contained courses in some 20 areas of study including English for the Foreign-Born, Begin-

seas. Captain Ruth A. Erickson, a graduate of the class of 1934, was named Chief of the Navy Nurse Corps in 1962.

As Rochester grew, so did its commitment to education, which was evident in the construction of new elementary, junior, and senior high schools. A sizable crowd gathered for the laying of the Coffman School cornerstone in 1910. Named in honor of the late Dr. L.D. Coffman, president of the University of Minnesota, the school served as Rochester's senior high school and was the home of Rochester State Junior College (RSJC) for 50 years. RSJC was founded in 1915 at the suggestion of Dr. Charles H. Mayo, who pro-ning Sign Language, Hardanger Embroidery, Small Engine Repair, and Parents Are Important In Rochester (PAIIR).

Winona State University opened its new building on the Rochester Community College campus in 1986. The two learning institutions joined forces to offer the "Two-Plus-Two" program, through which students can complete two years of study at each school to fulfill a four-year degree. In response to community needs, the initial courses focused on business and nursing education.

From the isolation of rural schools, educational opportunities now have grown to include vocational education, combined education (such as the program offered through Winona State University and Rochester Community College), focused education (such as the courses at the Olmsted County Historical Society), educational programs for senior citizens, and community education. Sanford Niles would have been pleased.

SIGNIFICANT DATES IN PUBLIC EDUCATION

1849   Organic Act of Territory of Minnesota authorizes state funding of public education.

1855   The Rochester School District is founded.

1856   First school is built in Rochester (a log schoolhouse).

1856   Olmsted County levies first school tax.

1857   Samuel G. Whiting files first school report.

1860   Town superintendents supervise schools.

1862   District examiners supervise schools.

1864   Board of Education is authorized.

1865   Sanford Niles is appointed superintendent of schools.

1865   First Teachers' Training Institute is held in Rochester.

1868   Central School is completed.

1945   First vocational classes are offered to adults.

1958   John Marshall High School opens.

1966   Mayo High School opens.

1974   Community Education is initiated by Independent School District 535.

1987   Winona State University and Rochester Community College join forces in the "Two-Plus-Two" Program.

1987   The Greater Rochester University Center Board is created. Rochester hosts its first Legislative Weekend for 83 state legislators in an effort to lobby for additional higher education.

David Granahan completed his Rochester Post Office mural in 1937. The primary colors of the mural seemed to be enhanced by the tan lobby walls. Note the stylized design of Granahan's mural and his careful hand shading. Courtesy, Olmsted County Historical Society

6

CIRCUSES AND SYMPHONIES

Starved for diversion, pioneers applauded any entertainment that managed to reach Rochester. John Stevens, a local sign painter, capitalized on this public need. Moved by Lavinia Eastlick's chilling tale of surviving the 1862 Shetek Indian massacre (Sioux Uprising), Stevens decided to depict the tragedy.

He painted a series of scenes— landscapes, aerial views, battle scenes, and portraits—in a primitive style. According to Bertha Heilbron in *Documentary Panorama*, Stevens discovered that a liberal use of red paint conveyed brutal realism. Stevens entered the pictures from his series in the La Crosse, Wisconsin, county fair. He won top awards. "Pretty good for our Rochester artist," hailed the *Rochester City Post* on October 21, 1865.

The inventive Stevens then glued his paintings onto a long canvas. He devised a roller mechanism, a forerunner of motion pictures, which slowly advanced the paintings. To further dramatize the massacre, Stevens wrote a script for his panorama. Captain C.E. Sencerbox, a Mississippi riverboat captain, was hired to "delineate" scenes. In 1868 Stevens' panorama made its debut at the St. Paul Opera House. Posters hailed the show as "The Most Extraordinary Exhibition in the World!"

But Stevens was ambitious and did not stop at St. Paul. He exhibited his panorama throughout Minnesota, Iowa, Wisconsin, and Illinois. Perhaps the constant rollings and re-rollings damaged the panorama. At least, Heilbron believed this explains why Stevens retired his first panorama and began work on a second in 1870. Stevens attempted to make his new paintings different from the first by using diluted, translucent colors. He called his technique "diaphanous painting."

Stevens even decorated the wagon that transported his panorama. Huge billboards, also painted by Stevens, were affixed to the sides of the wagon. To further advertise the panorama, Stevens put lights inside the wagon at night. In 1873 Stevens hired Merton Eastlick, Lavinia's son, who survived the massacre as a boy, to travel with the show. When Stevens accompanied the panorama, he reverted to his first career—painting signs on scrap lumber and posting them along roadsides.

Clearly, the sign painter had become a showman. "Stevens' success in the show business is not hard to explain," wrote Heilbron. "He understood and used with skill many tricks of advertising. He maintained interest in his panorama by picturing current events . . ." Rochester lawyer Burt Eaton saw the panorama as a boy and never forgot the experience.

In 1919 Eaton presented the Minnesota Historical Society with an original Stevens panorama. Eaton had spent months tracking down the 36 painted panels, wooden crates, roller mechanism, two kerosene lamp pedestals, and handwritten script. When fully extended the six-foot-high panorama stretched some 220 feet. Eaton sent directions along with his dona-

The Quilters Sew-Ciety was founded in 1977 to preserve the art of quilting. Members worked together to create this sampler quilt, sometimes called a legacy quilt, completed in 1980. The quilt was donated to the Olmsted County Historical Society. Courtesy, Olmsted County Historical Society

tion. Wrote Heilbron, "Eaton explained that 'the painted part of the panorama goes on the outside and when it is all run off then the crank is changed from the roller upon which it is used to operate the panorama to the other roller so that it can be re-rolled in the original position.'"

But the simple entertainment of John Stevens was eclipsed by circus glitter. As early as August 8, 1860, Cooke's Royal Circus pulled into Rochester. Mabie's Menagerie, a Twin Cities group, arrived in 1864, bringing with it elephants, lions, "and a full collection of wild beasts from the four ends of the earth," so posters claimed.

According to Dr. Robert J. Loeffler, author of "Visits of Circuses to the City of the Doctors Mayo," the first railroad circus arrived in Rochester in 1875. Advertisements for the circus promised an impressive production: 22 flat cars, 10 palace horse cars (each 36 feet long), 2 elephant cars (also 36 feet long), 4 boxcars, 3 sleeping cars, and one baggage car, for a total of 42 cars. "No more! No less," the ad said smugly.

Circus-goers were perhaps just as excited about seeing electricity at the Electric Light Circus, which arrived on July 10, 1879, as they were about seeing the show itself. Power for illuminating the circus tents, "as bright as day," according to the newspaper, came from a portable, 35-horsepower engine. The engine also powered a calliope which warbled "Baby Mine" and other toe-tapping favorites.

Barnum's Circus, not yet Barnum & Bailey's, rolled into Rochester in 1880. This troupe was followed by Cooper, Jackson & Company in 1882 with its thrilling cannon act. Spectators must have gasped collectively when the Great Zazel, a woman, was shot from a cannon. Ringling Brothers visited Rochester in 1891 and again in 1893, when they staged the first circus parade ever seen in Rochester. The *Rochester Post* estimated the cost of circus performances, including the parade, at a stunning one million dollars.

A May 31, 1894, advertisement in the *Olmsted County Democrat* listed Ringling Brothers' top acts: Caesar's Triumphal Entry into Rome, which the copy writer described as a "Dazzling Picture of Opulence and Splendor" ; Ludin, the strongest man in the world, who could easily lift 3,000 pounds while supporting a platform holding 20 men; the largest living giraffe; and a four-ton hippopotamus, billed as a "blood-sweating behemoth of the Nile."

Responding to the public's craving for circus news, the *Olmsted County Democrat* published a special circus supplement on June 14, 1894. The supplement detailed the history of Ringling Brothers, explained how performers started as youngsters, and acknowledged the hardships of circus life.

Occasionally a rowdy, dishonest circus played in Rochester. The *Post And Record* of July 10, 1903, panned one circus, describing the troupe as one of the most "disreputable, lawless and indecent bunches of humanity that ever struck Rochester." Loeffler's research uncovered evidence that the circus was running con games which bilked customers anywhere from $5 to $200. This negative publicity, however, did not quench the public's thirst for circus entertainment. Circuses became so popular that special train service from Zumbrota to Rochester was initiated in 1905 to transport circus-goers.

Shadow plays date back to the fourteenth century—perhaps earlier—and were a popular form of entertainment in the Rochester area. Shadow plays were simple entertainment that required few materials: cardboard for silhouettes (the ancient Turks also used leather), sticks to hold the silhouettes, white cloth, and a light source. An entire drama, usually one act, could be staged by a single narrator/ puppeteer. Refreshments and prizes added to the entertainment. "The shadow sociable at the ladies' parlors [in Oronoco] was a grand success," reported the *Rochester Post* on December 3, 1886.

On November 12, 1886, the *Record & Union* contained a notice for an upcoming Chinese shadow play titled "Ah Sin in Search of a Meal." Presented by the young people of Grace Church, the play

was billed as the best comic entertainment of the season. An admission fee of 10 cents was charged and refreshments were served.

Medicine shows toured the country from 1870 until about 1930. Countless shows passed through Rochester on their way to other midwestern towns, the most lucrative region for these shows. Brooks McNamara, author of *Step Right Up,* wrote: "The medicine shows cheerfully borrowed everything that was taking place elsewhere in the American theatre." Magic acts, burlesque, vaudeville, Punch and Judy shows, comedy, and miracle cures all were used to lure customers for the real purpose of the show—sales.

According to McNamara the staples of medicine shows were an herb compound, liniment, salve, cough medicine, and medicated soap. Many of these so-called remedies were concocted in hotel room bathtubs. Wizard Oil was a popular remedy, perhaps because of its ingredients: camphor, ammonia, chloroform, sassafras, cloves, and turpentine. Some batches of Wizard Oil contained from 55 to 70 percent alcohol, which may have prompted favorable press coverage in the *Post & Record* on September 11, 1869. "It is a regular concert saloon on wheels, with patent medicine substituted for the beer that is sold at the stationary entertainments of that kind," commented the reporter.

Kickapoo shows were a separate branch of medicine shows. John Healy, a slick door-to-door salesman, conceived the idea of marketing fake Indian medicine. Far from Indian country, Healy and two partners founded the Kickapoo Indian Medicine Company at 34th Street in New York City. The medicine was a simmered conglomeration of roots, barks, gums, herbs, leaves, and buffalo fat. The Indian White Cloud and his wife were Kickapoo performers. Some long-term Rochester residents speculate the couple lived in the city during the winter of 1929. Their speculation is based upon a single piece of evidence, a photograph of White Cloud and his wife taken by Abbott Studios of Rochester.

Members of the Wide Awake Glee Club stopped singing long enough to have their pictures taken. The club was founded in 1890 by a group of young students. After many years, spouses began to appear in club photographs. Effie Colligan, a high school music teacher, directed the group. Courtesy, Olmsted County Historical Society

In time Kickapoo shows faded and were replaced by band music. Several attempts had been made to organize a city band but with little success. Finally, the Rochester Musical Union was established in 1869. The group presented instrumental and vocal concerts. During the early 1870s, perhaps because of varying musical tastes, the union formed three separate groups: the Rochester Musical Union, Rochester Cornet Band, and Lovejoy Orchestra. Another musical group, the Rochester Park Band, was founded in 1894. Claude Coon was its first director, followed by Harold Cooke, a consummate musician who served the community in many ways.

Cooke, born on June 5, 1894, studied at the New England Conservatory of Music. He earned bachelor's and master's degrees from the MacPhail School of Music in Minneapolis. With his brother Glen, Cooke founded the Rochester Symphony in 1920. It was just the beginning of Cooke's career. He served as director of the Civic Music for 27 years, in addition to directing the Boychoir, Male Chorus, and the Rochester Park Band and Symphony Orchestra. Around 1949 the Civic Music program joined forces with city government and established an office at city hall.

Ralph Blakely, a fine musician, suggested to Dr. Will that a band shell be built for summer concerts. Dr. Will and Dr. Charlie liked the suggestion and do-

nated $15,500 to finance the band shell, which was built in 1915. Ellerbe and Rounds designed the shell, which had the same type of sounding boards used in organs. Musicians from the Minneapolis, Chicago, Detroit, St. Louis, and Kansas City orchestras were hired to play in the 10-week series of summer concerts.

One composition featured at concerts was the "Rochester Jubilee Hymn," written in 1929 by Harold Cooke and Thomas Magath, head of the Mayo Clinic laboratories. The stirring chorus raised gooseflesh:

May Rochester forever live
To be a blessing for mankind
A lovely place on Nature's face
Reflection of Man's heart and mind.

On his 80th birthday Cooke was proclaimed "Mr. Music" by the mayor of Rochester. Other musicians made their special kind of music. In 1892 the Loyal Temperance Legion assembled a small orchestra, if it could be called that. The *Olmsted County Democrat* noted on August 18, 1892, "Their orchestra consists of only four pieces but they are doing good work." On January 10, 1895, a notice appeared in the *Olmsted County Democrat* announcing the next rehearsal of the Queen City Guitar and Banjo Club. The group was either incredibly bad or incredibly cheap, for the notice concluded, "The public is cordially invited to stay away."

In an attempt to increase circulation, the *Rochester Post* decided to publish sheet music. The newspaper proudly announced its "gift of first-class music" on August 10, 1894. These complete works of music, obtained from the New York Musical Echo Company, were published on the newspaper's front page. "This music is by the best authors and composers in the country," declared the newspaper. "The songs are late and popular, the music of high grade, and the series will be well worth preserving."

Rochester's interest in music surged with construction of the Grand Opera House, located on the third floor of a building on the Heaney block. Originally built in 1866, the opera house was improved in 1867 with the addition of 200 seats. Later remodeling added 45 gas lamps and a new curtain. The curtain, which pictured an adoring young man gazing at a lovely young woman, became an attraction itself. Other patrons came to hear the new piano with a mandolin attachment, installed in 1896.

Movie equipment was installed in the Grand Opera House in 1900. Repertoire companies, however, continued to perform plays such as *East Lynn, Ten Nights in a Bar Room,* and *The Jack of Diamonds.* Melodrama troupes staged such thrillers as *Over Niagara Falls, The White Slave,* and *Tracked Across the Atlantic.* But melodramas and plays came to an abrupt halt when the theater burned down in 1917.

Another elegant theater, the Metropolitan, was completed in 1902. Patrons were awed by its lavish interior, red walls trimmed with golden scrolls, gold and cream ceiling, and proscenium sky effect. Some of the 1,000 theater seats were reserved on a permanent basis. The Metropolitan Theatre booked Shakespearean troupes and popular speakers of the day. Both William Jennings Bryan and Carry Nation made live appearances at the Metropolitan.

"Perhaps one of the first attempts of showing sound and camera, occurred in August 1908 when the Cameraphone made its first appearance here," wrote Grace Nye Wilson. *The Birth of a Nation* was shown at the Metropolitan Theatre in 1915. Like many other famous landmarks, the elegant Metropolitan fell victim to wrecking crews in 1936 when it was razed and replaced by a department store.

With the advent of motion pictures, a succession of movie theaters was built in Rochester. Like film frames clicking past the lens of history, the theaters quickly came and went: Dieter's Electric Theatre (1907), Dream Theatre, later renamed Bijou (1907), Majestic Theatre (1908), Empress Theatre (1914), Grand Theatre (1915), Garden Theatre (1916), Lawler Theatre (1916), and Chateau Dodge Theatre (1927).

M.L. Finklestein and I.H. Ruben were co-owners of the Chateau Dodge Theatre, a

Above: Workmen finished painting the interior of the Chateau Theatre at noon on the day of its opening in 1927. The theater was completely refurbished in 1976. Walls were repainted, decorative art work was carefully cleaned, and rocking seats were installed. Courtesy, Olmsted County Historical Society

Above right: Paul Whiteman played at the Chateau Theatre on August 28, 1939. Whiteman brought his entire 45-piece band with him, including the Four Modernaires, the Sax-soc-tette, and the Swinging Strings. The group was in Rochester one day only and played three performances. Courtesy, Olmsted County Historical Society

$400,000 theater built on the site of the former Dodge Lumber Company—hence its name. The opening program described the theater's ingenious electrical and ventilating systems and temperature control. What made the Chateau unique, though, was its charming decor, which the owners called "atmospheric."

Members of the audience must have felt as if they had been magically transported to a French village. Balconies and turrets decorated the front and sides of the 1,497-seat theater. Artificial flowers and clinging vines created irregular splashes of color on the hand-textured stucco walls. Overhead, puffy white clouds drifted past ever-twinkling stars. A massive Wurlitzer organ boomed out concerts.

The Chateau, as it came to be known, was equipped with 12 different backdrops and dressing rooms. Shakespearean plays were some of the first dramas staged at the Chateau, followed by vaude-

ville troupes and theater groups. *You Can't Take It with You,* by Moss Hart and George S. Kaufman, played at the Chateau. The movie classic *Gone with the Wind* played for one week in 1940.

Any discussion of theaters would be incomplete without mention of Mayo Auditorium, a gift of Dr. C.H. Mayo and the Mayo Properties Association to the city of Rochester. The tri-functional facility included an arena, a theater, and north and south exhibit halls. However, this was not the Mayos' only artistic gift to the city. Dr. Will and Dr. Charlie also donated a carillon to Mayo Clinic.

Dr. Will became fascinated with carillons while on a medical trip to England. When he returned, Dr. Will asked Ellerbe architects to revise the Plummer Building plans to accommodate a carillon. A handsome tower was added to the previously flat-topped building. Twenty-three bells, weighing 36,988 pounds, were cast at the Johnson Foundry in Croydon, England, which specialized in bell metal. On August 16, 1928, Dr. Will and Dr. Charlie dedicated the Mayo Clinic carillon to the American soldier. In 1977 an additional 33 bells were added to the carillon, for a total of 56 bells. The bells were the gift of Frances Sheets and Isabella Gooding Sanders, descendants of early Rochester pioneer Alphonso Gooding.

Rochester composer Orvis Ross still lives in the memories of those who knew him. Ross was born in Pipestone on December 14, 1894. He studied music at the American Conservatory in Chicago. The struggling pianist lived in New York City during the 1920s. Ross' landlord was, of all people, writer Henry Miller. If Miller was busy, Ross escorted Miller's wife to concerts and plays. The April 12, 1978, edition of the *Rochester Post-Bulletin* ran an article about their friendship entitled "Orvis Ross in New Book about Friends of Henry Miller." Miller recalled his friendship with Ross in a chapter about bike riding: "What we shared together is unforgettable. He [Ross] enriched my life indelibly."

After World War I Ross established a music school in Mankato. He served as the Hamline University chapel organist from 1930 to 1933. In 1935 Ross moved to Rochester to work as an accompanist for silent movies. The following year Ross became conductor of the Rochester Symphony, a post he held until 1942. In 1946 the First Universalist Church hired Ross as its music director. Management duties did not deter Ross from giving piano and organ lessons, conducting, and composing.

Ross composed a broad range of music, from sacred to secular, from choral works to symphonies, from solos to orchestral pieces. Ross often composed pieces for his students. But it was *The Crescent Moon*, a concert-length composition dedicated to his mother, that became Ross' lifetime work. "He spent at least 35 years revising it," recalled Dr. Bruce Douglass, former symphony board president. "Orvis never seemed to be fully satisfied with the way it stood." Because of these endless revisions, *The Crescent Moon* was never published. Only handwritten copies of the composition exist, treasured by the Rochester musicians who have them.

Charlotte Douglass, music teacher and pianist, characterized Ross' work as romantic. "Sometimes I thought it was Puccini-like," she said. Complex, often dissonant, chords were Ross' musical signature. Key changes occurred in his music with the smooth liquidity of flowing water. Performers often cringed at the chords but were, nonetheless, fascinated by the composer's talent.

Another Rochester artist, of a different medium, Nicholas Brewer had so much talent he became a painter of presidents. His family settled along the banks of the Root River in an area known as High Forest, and Brewer was born in 1857. Like any other farm boy, Brewer did chores including milking, plowing, and breaking horses. His real dream, however, was to become a painter. In his autobiography, *Trails of a Paintbrush*, Brewer described how, as an eight-year-old boy, he painted farm subjects.

At age 18, frustrated by his lack of technical skill, Brewer decided to leave home to pursue art training in St. Paul. Brew-

Orvis Ross was a gifted Rochester composer who gave his music as gifts. When invited for dinner, Ross often appeared at the front door with original sheet music in hand, written especially for his host and hostess. Thus, many Ross compositions exist as single manuscript copies— personalized works to be savored. Courtesy, First Unitarian Universalist Church

er's parents could not afford to finance his college education, but they did provide their son with the proceeds from a load of wheat. So the ambitious Brewer arrived in St. Paul with $34 in his pocket.

Henry J. Koempel gave Brewer painting lessons for 50 cents apiece. Brewer was eyeing more than his teacher's paintings: three years later he married Koempel's daughter, Rose. Lack of funds did not seem to diminish the couple's happiness, though Brewer worked hard to earn a living. He gave crayon lessons and painted on almost anything available— wagons, houses, and fences. The determined Brewer taught himself how to simulate oak graining, a skill in high demand at the time. Between odd jobs Brewer perfected his portrait-painting skills by copying photographs.

Brewer took painting lessons from two New York City artists, but his lessons were brief and he remained largely self-taught. Portrait painting fascinated him, and he wrote in his diary, "The painted portrait is the voice of the soul speaking through features." Surely, Brewer glimpsed some famous souls when he painted Ulysses S. Grant, Grover Cleveland, and Franklin D. Roosevelt. "I think I was fortunate in choosing Roosevelt's profile with the head slightly elevated," said Brewer. "I avoided the least hint of his characteristic smile."

Readers probably smiled when Brewer's autobiography was published in 1938. But like Sanford Niles, Brewer's name and work seem to have faded into the mists of time.

The Depression of the 1930s provided work for national and local artists. On October 16, 1934, Henry Morgenthau, secretary of the treasury, signed an executive order creating the Section of Painting and Sculpture. This order launched a national campaign to identify and reward artists. "His [Morgenthau's] far-flung plan for artistic development in this country . . . was to secure for the government the best art which this country is capable of producing, with merit as the only test," wrote Forbes Watson. Watson served as editor of the *Bulletin: Section of Painting and Sculpture,* published monthly.

Artist David Granahan, a Litchfield native, was the recipient of a national award. Granahan was selected to paint a mural for the Rochester Post Office. Intrigued with the story of Henrietta Head dragging a log to clear Broadway, Granahan selected the folklore incident as the topic of his three-paneled mural.

Granahan attended the Minneapolis School of Art. Guggenheim fellowships enabled him to do postgraduate work abroad. He also did postgraduate work at the Minneapolis School of Art and the Chicago Art Institute. After completing the mural, Granahan and his wife, a painter who signed her work under the name of Lolita Wadman, personally installed it in the post office.

The couple worked from 7 A.M. until 10 P.M. applying glue to the post office wall and stretching canvases to fit the wall dimensions. Lolita Granahan smoothed the canvases with a rolling pin to remove any wrinkles or air bubbles. Postal patrons observed the Granahans' scaffold work with interest. The *Rochester Post-Bulletin* reported on October 3, 1937, "To make the paintings exactly fit these sections, it was necessary for Mr. Granahan to trim slightly the heavy canvas, on which the mural is painted. The paintings, which he did in his studios in the Walker Art Galleries, were carefully rolled and shipped here by express in a sturdy wooden box."

Mayo Foundation acquired the old post office buildings in 1974 under provisions of a land-swap arrangement with the General Services Administration. Mayo Clinic needed the land for a parking lot. The Olmsted County Historical Society thought it had three months to ponder how to safely remove Granahan's mural from the post office. Suddenly, the demolition date for the building was advanced.

Just one day before the arrival of the wrecking crew, Brad Linder, director of the society, found himself standing on a scaffold and wielding a putty knife. "Starting at the top, we carefully scraped the canvas loose," said Linder in a *Rochester Post-Bulletin* article. "We had to be careful not to tear the paintings, of course." Gingerly the three panels were wound around large carpet tubes. Linder and his crew were successful. Today the mural hangs in the main exhibit hall of the Olmsted County Historical Society.

Granahan continued to view his work through a historical perspective. On December 9, 1978, he wrote to the historical society's archivist about his mural. Granahan, approaching 86 years of age, said he had not realized his mural had been removed from the post office and rehung at the historical center. He continued in a faltering hand, "It is all hard for people of this time and age to realize what hardships, a hard life [it was] to live thru the early days of the state of Minn."

Newton Holland, a superb painter himself, appreciated local art and artists. So Holland organized an Art Center, which staged its initial exhibitions at the public library. In 1948 the group moved into the German Methodist church. But the building always remained a rather dark, partitioned church, an atmosphere that hardly enhanced the exhibits. In 1957 groundbreaking ceremonies were held for the new Art Center, a $65,000 cement block building located in Mayo Park.

Holland was unable to attend the ceremony because of illness. But he sent a written message that read, in part, "Rochester is unique in the country among the cities of comparable population to have such splendid quarters to house its arts program." More than 1,000 people attended the opening exhibit at the Art Center. Holland was selected president of the Rochester Art Center Board. In his report Holland noted, "We feel that our exhibitions have been of high order, have been handsomely staged, and have been well attended."

The Art Center attracted visitors and sponsored activities such as speakers, teaching programs, and buffet suppers. The work of the Art Center's first director, William Saltzman, also attracted attention.

Newt Holland catches up on paperwork in his cafeteria. Customers flocked to Holland's for good food and interesting art, displayed in The Little Gallery. Courtesy, Olmsted County Historical Society

Saltzman graduated from the University of Minnesota, taught at Macalester College, and was assistant director of the University of Minnesota Galleries when approached by the Rochester Art Center.

Besides managing the Art Center, Saltzman taught three days a week and served as artist-in-residence. Interestingly, Saltzman's abstract work became more realistic while he lived in Rochester. Saltzman believed strongly in community involvement. "There should be millions of art centers," he said. "You can't have it a club—I think we tried to develop broad community interest."

Community interest in the arts virtually exploded. By 1970 more than 300 arts activities were held in Rochester annually. To coordinate these myriad activities the Rochester Area Council for the Arts (RACA) was founded. Bylaws for the council stated, "Membership is open to organizations and individuals involved in the arts and supportive of the arts in the Rochester area." RACA activities included quarterly meetings and workshops.

Mayo Clinic owns the most extensive art collection in southeastern Minnesota. Since the Romanesque-style Plummer Building was erected in 1928, art has been a top priority at Mayo. According to *Mirror to Man: The Murals at Mayo Clinic,* a Mayo Clinic brochure, the official art program began in the 1950s in order to provide an artistic environment

Charles Gagnon: Internationally Acclaimed Sculptor

Renaissance Woman is one of two sculptures Charles Gagnon created for Kenyon College. Gagnon, a Rochester resident, supervises the on-site installations of his work. "I'm with my sculptures all the way," explains Gagnon. But once Renaissance Man and Woman were installed, Gagnon found he missed them. So Gagnon and his wife, Arlyn, make "annual pilgrimages" to Gambier, Ohio. Courtesy, Charles Gagnon

Rochester residents unfamiliar with the art world may not realize Charles Gagnon, an internationally acclaimed sculptor, resides in their midst. Why does Gagnon live in Rochester? "Rochester is, for me, a very fine environment in which to work," explains Gagnon. And while Gagnon savors all seasons, he finds special beauty in winter, when snow covers sculptures and trees. "Winter is an essential part of my life," says Gagnon. "I'm always sad when those incredibly beautiful snow forms leave."

His studio is an integral part of Gagnon's home, which is a sculpture in itself. Gagnon shares the studio with his wife, Arlyn, also an artist, whom he met while she was serving as interim director of the Rochester Art Center. Arlyn's pastels, watercolors, and colored pencil drawings are at one end of the studio; Charles' sculptures are at the other.

At first Gagnon, unused to the spaciousness of his new 77-foot skylit studio, tended to work in a small corner. No more. His sculptures soar toward the 35-foot ceiling, which is delineated by a massive steel beam. A block and tackle dangle from one end of the beam. Gagnon works with clay, wax, and plaster models, along with some bronze finishing. All of his sculptures are cast at a foundry in New York.

Gagnon was born in Minneapolis on February 14, 1934. He earned three master's degrees in fine arts from the University of Minnesota and did six years of postgraduate work in Europe. Gagnon considers himself fortunate to have studied with Jacques Lipchitz, whom he met in Italy in 1965. Lipchitz saw something in Gagnon's work—a hint of what he was to become. "You have the gift," Lipchitz told Gagnon. The two sculptors corresponded until Lipchitz's death in 1973.

Working on simultaneous projects is essential to Gagnon. "The concentration is so intense that after a period of time you lose sight of many things, good and bad, that are transpiring," he explains. Gagnon thinks these simultaneous projects help him to maintain objectivity. Lesser works are changed—occasionally destroyed—something Gagnon has

for patients and staff. The Mayo Clinic art collection can be classified into broad categories such as ceramics, paintings, sculpture, tapestries, and original prints. International art, such as the Mayo Foundation Pre-Columbian Collection, donated by Seymour Rosenberg, forms a category of its own.

Two modern works, Yaakov Agam's mobile *Welcome* and David Wynne's sculpture *Boy with a Dolphin,* represent the Mayo Clinic's growing interest in contemporary art. Agam, an Israeli artist, said the purpose of this work was to welcome people with an optimistic, visual smile. From the day it was installed in the Mayo Building lobby, Agam's kinetic mobile has fascinated the public. Adorned with thousands of geometric patterns, the electronically controlled mobile makes a complete rotation approximately every three minutes.

David Wynne, a British artist, described *Boy with a Dolphin* as a work of trust. "The boy is being shown that if you trust the world, the thrills and great happiness are yours," he said. Wynne's sculpture is not only a work of beauty, it is an engineering marvel. Roland, Wynne's youngest son, was the model for the work. The sculpture was presented to Mayo Clinic by Count and Countess Theo and Ida Rossi di Montelara of Geneva, Switzerland

Actors presented their talents to the community through the theater. The Roches-

learned from experience. "I wouldn't finish or cast any of my sculptures into bronze unless I felt it was the very best that is within me," he explains.

During the last 30 years Gagnon has created several hundred sculptures. *Saint Francis and the Birds*, weighing one ton, was commissioned by St. Marys Hospital in Rochester. *Renaissance Man and Woman*, which stands 10 feet high, was commissioned by Kenyon College in Gambier, Ohio. Other Gagnon sculptures may be found in Canada, Japan, South America, England, and other parts of Europe. In 1976 Gagnon was listed in *Who's Who in American Art*, *Who's Who in the Midwest*, and *Who's Who in America*.

According to Gagnon, ideas are the most important aspect of the creative process. Gagnon hopes his sculptures will inspire future generations. He has designed one peace sculpture and plans to do others. "I love the theme of peace," he says quietly, "one person to another, one family to another, neighbor to neighbor, community, city, state, countries, and the universe."

ter Civic Theatre was founded during the summer of 1951. Its first thespians performed in the Izaak Walton League Cabin, so locals referred to the group as the Log Cabin Theatre. The theater group expanded and moved productions to an old building off Broadway. Again the group's name was changed to fit its location, to The Little Theatre Off Broadway. But the building, which some remember as an old laundry, was not suitable for performances.

As the Civic Theatre's fund-raising brochure stated so honestly, "This building at 6 N.W. 7th Street was never intended or designed for theatrical use. It has variously been a bottling plant, a truck garage, and a heating appliance warehouse." Inadequate storage, office space, and restrooms made productions difficult. Fund-raising efforts for a new theater were successful. Civic Theatre moved into its new Mayo Park location in 1963 and opened the season with *South Pacific.*

Countless Rochester artists, fiddlers, quilters, bell ringers, clog dancers, set designers, poets, weavers, whittlers, and more have enriched the lives of those around them. Most of these artists have remained unknown. A precious few have achieved fame. Over the years these artists crafted Rochester's artistic identity, an identity so strong that the city's name has become synonymous with the word art.

It's time for lift-off at the Mayor's Cup Invitational Hot Air Balloon Race, held in conjunction with Rochesterfest 1987. Twenty pilots entered the contest, inflating their balloons on the green adjacent to John Adams Junior High School. Photo by Jerry Olson. Courtesy, Rochester Post-Bulletin

7

ROCHESTER SHAPES AND SPIRIT

"Rochester is coming into line as a summer resort, and rightfully so, for a more picturesque and homelike place does not exist in Minnesota," reported the *Olmsted County Democrat* on April 21, 1892. Businessmen had begun to market Rochester as a resort city. But the rivers and creeks that contributed to Rochester's beauty were the same ones which flooded repeatedly, destroying property and sometimes lives.

Visitors and residents were all affected, one way or another, by the 1978 flood. The swollen rivers were already threatening the city's safety when a thunderstorm struck at 7:30 on the evening of July 5. Six inches of rain fell during the night, turning meandering streams such as Bear Creek into raging torrents of water. An estimated 5,000 residents had to be evacuated from their homes.

Around town the sounds of explosions were heard as transformers and power lines connected with rising floodwaters. Power failures forced St. Marys and Methodist hospitals to operate on emergency generators. In total, five people were killed—four were residents of a local nursing home who died when they were trapped in an elevator. Throughout the night the *Rochester Post-Bulletin* was without power. At 9 A.M. power was restored, computers were partially operational by 10:30, and the newspaper managed to publish an abbreviated edition.

Rochester woke up to a sun-drenched morning. The stark contrast to the previous night seemed to magnify the flood damage. Foundations of some homes had been partially swept away. Both Civic Theatre and K mart were under water. Apache Mall and Crossroads shopping centers had sustained minimal flood damage due to sandbagging, but damage nevertheless. Silver Lake shopping center was severely damaged. And the stench of sludge—homogenized river mud and raw sewage—hung over the city.

Rochester Post-Bulletin reporter Ron Freeberg wrote on July 6 that hope, prayer, and sweat had kept the city's strained utilities operational. Utility crews had managed to protect the Rochester power plant by scooping huge piles of coal around it. Water swirled around the plant and raced toward Silver Lake, erasing its boundaries. Damaged water and natural gas systems were deemed safe by midmorning. The sewage plant, however, was out of commission and forced to dump into the Zumbro River. Mayor Alex Smekta estimated the flood damage at a mind-boggling $40 million.

Worse yet, the weather forecast predicted thunderstorms and locally heavy rain.

Community members and groups immediately galvanized into action. Assistance was provided by the Minnesota Civil Air Patrol, 934th Tactical Airlift Group (Air Force Reserves based in Minneapolis), Disabled American Veterans, National Guard, and Minnesota Division of Natu-

ral Resources, to name a few. Businesses offered their help, among them, Mayo Clinic, which approved 6,200 hours of time off (a total of $50,000 in salary costs) for employees who were flood victims. In addition, Mayo Clinic donated $50,000 to the Red Cross Disaster Relief Fund.

The July 7, 1978, edition of the *Rochester Post-Bulletin* contained a map of the flood area, an inverted-Y shape which stretched between Mayowood in the southwest, Bear Creek in the southeast, and Silver Lake in the northwest, and spilled over to the state hospital in the southeast. Bear Creek crested at 23½ feet over flood stage and the Zumbro River at 23 feet over flood stage. A fastfood restaurant taped to its window a parody of an antacid slogan which read, "How do you spell relief? Federal."

Federal assistance was needed—a bill that would solve Rochester's flood problem once and for all. With new resolve, members of the community worked for flood legislation. The U.S. Department of the Army, District Corps of Engineers based in St. Paul conducted an extensive

Dave Fritts steers his boat down Third Avenue S.E. during the 1978 flood. Fritts was one of several Rochester residents who used his boat to aid flood victims. Additional assistance came from the Department of Natural Resources, which donated the use of six boats. Courtesy, Rochester Post-Bulletin

study of Rochester flood control. In its 1978 *Revised Final Impact Statement,* the corps recommended 9.3 miles of channel modifications, supplemental levees, continued flood insurance, floodplain regulations, 20 miles of hiking and biking trails, 4 new parks, 7 upstream reservoirs, and land treatment measures.

Republican senator David Durenberger introduced the flood-control legislation in 1978 with bipartisan support. But federal financing of flood control was an ongoing, complicated, budgetary process—a waiting game. From 1978 to 1986 not one flood-control bill was passed. In a dramatic move, Rochester voters approved a one percent sales tax—raising the local tax to 7 percent—to finance flood control and build a much-needed civic center.

"The tax, first formally proposed in a memo from City Finance Director Paul Utesch to the Rochester Park Board in 1982, was heralded as a creative way of

---

ROCHESTER'S FLOOD HISTORY

Date	Measurement
July 6, 1978	23.00 feet
June 21, 1974	16.86 feet
May 1, 1973	13.36 feet
March 11, 1973	15.34 feet
April 4, 1969	11.17 feet
June 15, 1967	11.12 feet
March 27, 1967	11.45 feet
March 11, 1967	12.45 feet
March 4, 1966	14.94 feet
February 9, 1966	13.93 feet
April 6, 1965	13.55 feet
March 1, 1965	19.12 feet
March 29, 1962	18.46 feet
March 26, 1961	15.43 feet
June 4, 1958	13.54 feet
October 18, 1955	18.00 feet
June 19, 1954	11.21 feet
June 24, 1952	11.60 feet
March 31, 1952	13.26 feet
July 21, 1951	17.50 feet
June 23, 1908	18.00 feet

Source: *Rochester Post-Bulletin,* July 6, 1978, page 3. Statistics have been reordered chronologically

---

avoiding the need to fund the facility with property tax revenue," reported Bruce Marshall in "Civic Center Celebration," a special September 9, 1986, insert in the *Rochester Post-Bulletin.* Added Marshall, "The tax contains a sunset provision which repeals the tax as the arena and flood control projects are funded."

Rochester voters passed the sales tax referendum with a 60 percent vote. Because of a 1971 tax law that prohibited cities from having their own sales tax, the Minnesota legislature dragged its feet on approval of the measure. After testimony and much debate, the omnibus tax bill was passed on the final day of the 1983 legislative session. Twenty-four million dollars would be collected in taxes to pay off bonds and interest charges which funded the construction, remodeling, and floodproofing of Mayo Civic Center.

Finally, the Water Resources Development Act was passed in 1986. Public Law 99-662, part of the Water Resources Development Act, authorized flood control within and around Rochester, including the South Fork of the Zumbro River Project.

Rochester's downtown had been in need of renovation for decades and this

Evelyn Royce was only one of the countless volunteers who helped victims of the 1978 flood. Royce and coworkers packaged sandwiches at the Red Cross Center established at John Marshall High School. About 625 people were housed in local shelters. And, 17 members of the National Red Cross staff flew, or drove, to Rochester to assist relief workers. Photo by Nancy Pierce. Courtesy, Rochester Post-Bulletin

need, among others, prompted Rochester Area Chamber of Commerce executive vice president Mark Ricker to propose the FutureScan 2000 effort. A community strategic-planning process that involved more than 300 people, FutureScan 2000 was established to chart and plan for the most critical issues Rochester would face by the year 2000.

One of these issues was, of course, downtown redevelopment, and the Future-Scan 2000 redevelopment task force was given an almost impossible assignment. According to an October 11, 1986, article in the *Rochester Post-Bulletin*, the task force's mission was to "create and sustain a vibrant, exciting downtown Rochester for Mayo Clinic patients, downtown residents, city visitors, and convention center guests, all for the benefit of the community."

Four key issues were identified: use of space; entertainment and activities; transportation; and people. After studying these issues an additional five high-priority recommendations were made. These recommendations involved creating a downtown plan, constructing a skyway system, formulating plans for a joint government services campus, promoting downtown attractions, and developing a sign system to direct people to major destinations.

Al Tuntland, FutureScan 2000 chairman, said, "It is only right that this community now begin to make a significant investment in itself. We can no longer continue a childlike dependence on IBM and the Mayo Clinic." At the dedication of the Mayo Civic Center, Tuntland expressed hope for the future of downtown. "Rochester is on a roll and FutureScan, because of its unique composition as a public-private partnership, is in a perfect position to be the vehicle for facilitating our progress," said Tuntland.

On November 9, 1987, groundbreaking ceremonies were held for the Center Place project, a total renovation of the downtown area estimated to cost $44 million. The project's two major developers, William Maddux of Minneapolis and Gus Cha-

foulias of Rochester, were on hand for the event. Plans for Center Place included a luxury hotel, nine-story office complex, enclosed shopping center, and skyways. In short, 20 years of construction would be compressed into two. Mayor Chuck Hazama described Center Place as a "clear vision of what we want to be in the 21st century."

The renovation began with a vengeance. Downtown streets were torn up with such speed that the area resembled a war zone. Rochester became a city of jarring sounds, thumping wrecking balls, whirring cement mixers, pounding jackhammers, and grinding dump trunks, not to mention dynamite blasts. Never say the folks in Rochester don't have a sense of humor. Residents began referring to Rochester as the "holy city" in honor of the cavernous holes being dug by giant earth movers, or the "crane city" in honor of the many cranes which were silhouetted against the skyline.

Construction became the biggest show in town. Mayo Clinic recognized this fact and placed bleachers across from the construction site of its new education building. Patients became unofficial construction supervisors, gasping as cranes swiveled overhead and bulldozers chugged three stories below ground. Named the Harold W. Siebens Building in honor of a generous benefactor, the education building was just one of Mayo Clinic's expansion projects.

Satellite clinics were built in Jacksonville, Florida, and Scottsdale, Arizona. A dish antenna on top of the Mayo building enabled staff members to examine patients, confer with their colleagues, and instantly study test results, reported *The Mayo Alumnus*. Dr. Eugene Mayberry, then chief executive officer of Mayo Foundation, called the telecommunications system "the glue that will tie all our sites together."

On October 1, 1981, Mayo Clinic launched its Air Medical Transport Service—the Mayo 1 helicopter. A helipad was located on top of the Mary Brigh Building at St. Marys Hospital. Most of the helicopter's flights were within a 30- to 75-mile radius of Rochester. According to the September 1987 issue of *Mayovox*, the majority of Mayo 1 patients were trauma cases and cardiac-related emergencies. A significant number of newborn babies and high-risk maternal patients also were transported.

Mayo 1 has a standby crew of three pilots and a lead pilot, as well as nine flight nurses and a chief flight nurse. Within five minutes of dispatch the crew is airborne. By July 31, 1987, Mayo 1 had transported 1,290 patients. Rochester residents became accustomed to hearing the

Left: These construction workers are working on Mayo Clinic's new education building. Photo by Jim Welch. Courtesy, Rochester Post-Bulletin

Below: A helicopter was used to hoist Mayo Clinic's dish antenna atop the building. The system operates on an ultra-high frequency band, called KU, which transmits at 14,000 megahertz. Mayo Clinic's telecommunications is the first of its kind used to support a clinical practice. Courtesy, Mayo Clinic

Facing page: The renovation of downtown Rochester is clearly visible in this aerial photograph. As the cranes were assembled and raised, construction workers flew flags from them. Each week the Rochester Post-Bulletin published a map of the downtown area showing which streets were opened and which were closed. Photo by Jim Welch. Courtesy, Rochester Post-Bulletin

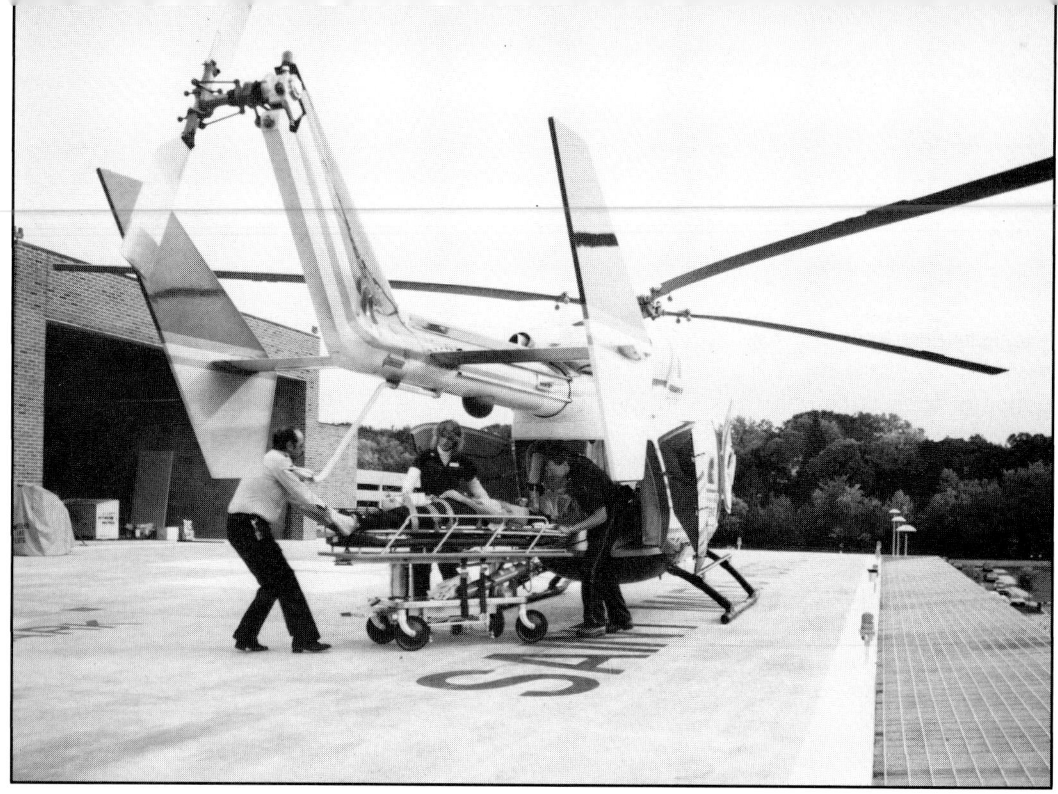

Right: Three members of the Mayo 1 helicopter crew remove a patient from the aircraft. Mayo Clinic's Air Transport Service began operations in 1984. Since that time Mayo 1 has averaged 50 flights per month. Mayo 1 can transport two adult patients simultaneously. Five percent of the helicopter's flights involve landing at an accident site. Courtesy, Mayo Clinic

Facing page, top: Two Native Americans, Dick Flores (left) and Nakoma Volkman (right), wear sharply contrasting outfits at a powwow in 1987. Courtesy, Rochester Post-Bulletin

Facing page, bottom: Charlie Garnet was one of the few blacks living in Rochester during 1896. Here Garnet drives the June wedding party of Frank Falkner and Edith Keifer. Courtesy, Olmsted County Historical Society

helicopter's whirring blades overhead, especially during the summer, its busiest time.

An emergency helicopter was one thing, but a Federal Medical Center to treat prison inmates was quite another.

When news of a proposed Federal Medical Center hit the pages of the *Rochester Post-Bulletin*, not everyone was pleased. Residents who were concerned about security and devaluation of property banded together to form the Olmsted Citizens for a Better Community (OCBC). For months the Rochester community was polarized into pro and con groups. OCBC's efforts were unsuccessful. The Olmsted County Board accepted the federal proposal for use of six buildings and 64 acres of land by a 4-to-1 vote. On May 1, 1984, the *Rochester Post-Bulletin* reported the sale of the former Rochester State Hospital campus to the Federal Bureau of Prisons. A photograph of the $14-million check, the purchase price, appeared on the front page.

Target capacity of the Federal Medical Center (FMC) was 500 inmates. The FMC opened its doors in October 1984 with 19 inmates. This figure increased to approximately 75 inmates the following year, and by 1987 the facility had reached capacity with 513 inmates. The *Rochester Post-Bulletin* of November 9, 1987, reported that most of them were general population inmates with no particular medical needs. Some received psychiatric and surgi-

cal care. Other inmates awaiting transfer were also housed at the FMC. Today the Federal Medical Center sits in the midst of what is called the Olmsted County Human Services Campus.

Service agencies became aware that faces in Rochester were changing. Three population groups were responsible for the change: Native Americans, blacks, and Southeast Asians. These groups not only altered the collective visage of Rochester but enriched the city's daily life.

By 1987 some 91 Indians resided in Olmsted County. Tracking and interpreting Indian population statistics is difficult because of how the ethnic group Indian is defined. Minnesota's legal definition of Indian was any individual of not less than one-quarter Indian blood. A state commission revised this definition in 1967 to "Indians duly enrolled with any Indian group." To further complicate matters, there were people who chose to accept Indian customs, traditions, beliefs, and tribal life.

Members of various Indian tribes, 300 strong, founded the Native American Center of Southeast Minnesota (NAC) in 1985. The group had one fervent purpose—to educate the general population. Reported an NAC powwow program member, "One of the real concerns was the misconceptions and time-worn stereotypes that the general public holds about American Indians."

Marguerite Mullaney described a powwow in the April 11, 1987, edition of the

Rochester Post-Bulletin. She defined a pow-wow as "the turning of a cycle, the resurgence of their tribal cultures and identities." Attendees were urged to ask questions about Indian beadwork and the meaning of the red eagle feather. "America doesn't have to be a melting pot. It should be a mosaic of all people maintaining their cultures," Nakoma Volkman was quoted as saying.

NAC gave school programs, sponsored bowling teams, formed the Bear Creek Singers, held costume-making and beadwork sessions, and produced a video in conjunction with Group W Cable. All of these activities helped to increase the public's understanding of Indian ways. "Tested by tragedy and born out of the will of the people to survive oppression, these dynamic new efforts promise to enrich not only tribal life but American society and culture as well," noted *They Chose Minnesota: A Survey of the State's Ethnic Groups.*

When the 1860 census was taken, no blacks were living in Olmsted County. The October 12, 1861, edition of the *Rochester City Post* contained a notice regarding education for blacks: "The Superintendent of Public Instruction, sustained by the Attorney General, has decided that the trustees of Districts have no right to exclude colored children from a full participation in the benefits of the common School system of the State." The black population increased imperceptibly, and by 1880 there were 11 blacks living in Rochester. Many of them had menial jobs.

Census figures listed blacks' occupations as laborer(s), veterinary surgeon, bakery-restaurant owner, hackman, housekeeper, saloonkeeper, and miller. The *Olmsted County Democrat* reported on March 3, 1911, that "Henry Smith, a colored gentlemen who has been employed in the city for the past year, last night entertained members of the 'Sunny South' show troupe at his home on Kansas Avenue. The occasion was one of the first ever held in this city, and was strictly a dark party." As prejudicial as this statement was, it acknowledged the existence of blacks.

Blacks who visited the city had difficulty in finding lodging. Verne Manning came to Rochester for medical treatment and experienced the problem firsthand. Manning later sold his Seattle, Washington, delicatessen; moved to Rochester; and opened the Avalon Hotel in 1944. Located on Broadway, Manning's hotel became a haven for black entertainers such as Duke Ellington and the Ink Spots.

Ron Freeberg, a *Rochester Post-Bulletin* staff writer, reported in a June 13, 1973, article that the Manning family had difficulty in gaining acceptance at first. The Manning children, however, eased the situation. "The kids got along well in school even though they were the only blacks for years," Manning was quoted as saying. Passage of antidiscrimination legislation opened the doors for blacks in Rochester. Manning sold his hotel in 1977, and it was converted into an apartment house.

Most of the blacks who came to Rochester were professionals, employed at either IBM or Mayo Clinic. However, in 1987 some members of the black community noticed a shift in demographics. More nonprofessionals were moving to Rochester. Less educated than their predecessors, these black workers had difficulty in finding top-level jobs. And some blacks reported they had been victims of housing discrimination.

In 1981 the Community Housing Resource Board was formed to handle complaints. Earl McGee, an IBM employee, agreed to serve as chairperson of the board. Board members, 15 in all, represented a cross-section of business, banking, and real estate groups. McGee told the *Rochester Post-Bulletin* that the Community Housing Board would handle complaints before they progressed through the court conciliation process, as reported in the paper on January 16, 1981.

The collective experience of blacks in Minnesota, and Rochester in particular, is more than a history of assimilation. "It has been an account of collective struggle against prejudice and discrimination led by individuals whose perseverance in the cause of justice and equality improved the quality of life for all Minnesotans," reported Dr. David V. Taylor in the study guide for the film, *Committees of One: The Black Experience in Minnesota.*

The Southeast Asians are Rochester's newest pioneers. Of the estimated 135,000 Indochinese (Vietnamese, ethnic Chinese, Hmong, Laotians, and Cambodians) who arrived in the United States during 1975, roughly 4,500 settled in Minnesota according to *They Chose Minnesota: A Survey of the State's Ethnic Groups.* The influx of refugees peaked between 1975 and 1981.

In 1975 Governor Wendell R. Anderson established the Indochinese Task Force. Two years later the Minnesota Department of Public Welfare assumed the duties of the task force and contracted with voluntary and professional agencies for assistance. A variety of groups provided assistance in Rochester including Church

Chhoern Lam and her five-year-old daughter, Sopea, huddle under an umbrella while waiting for the bus to come. The Lams were accustomed to rain, but probably unprepared for the gusting winds in Rochester, the eighth-windiest city in the nation. Photo by Jim Welch. Courtesy, Rochester Post-Bulletin

World Service, Lutheran Social Service, and Catholic Charities, which became the official resettlement headquarters. Assistance was also provided by the Rochester Refugee Resettlement Association, a volunteer group.

Why did the refugees come to Rochester? Community willingness to sponsor the refugees was one reason. Some refugees came because they had family members living here. Others wanted to live near natives from their homeland. Availability of community services, including those of Independent School District 535, was another reason. Finally, refugees with medical problems knew they would find competent care in Rochester.

Once they arrived in Rochester the refugees not only experienced culture shock but were exposed—literally—to weather shock. One child recalled his shock at seeing snow. "When we got off the plane there was white everywhere," he said. "It was cold." The Southeast Asians, many coming from temperate climates, were psychologically and physically unprepared for subzero weather. Certainly they were unfamiliar with long underwear, knitted hats, face masks, thermal mittens, and snowmobile boots.

Grocery stores began to carry some ethnic foods such as bok choy, but did not have the array of fresh vegetables which composed the refugees' preferred diet. Most Southeast Asians were unfamiliar with dairy products, and considered milk, butter, and cheese to be strange, if not sickening, foods. Nor did they know what to do with the products stocked on foodbank shelves. Dietary problems, however, were minor compared to the real life horrors most refugees had endured.

The children's stories were so horrific that the secretary who typed them for Sherry Bierbaum, coordinator of the Limited English Proficiency Program, cried as she did so. One child wrote about his departure from Vietnam:

I sat on a bench outside my house with my grandmother. She told me I had to take care of my mother and younger brothers and sister. If

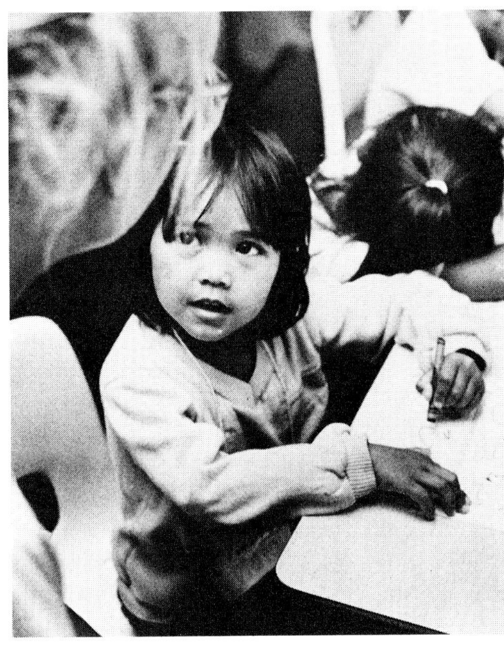

Malay Tuon, pre-kindergarten student, is hard at work in the Limited English Proficiency Program (LEP). Seventy children participated in the program during August 1987. Courtesy, Rochester Post-Bulletin

I worked hard in the U.S. and did well in school, she would be with me in spirit.

Around midnight we went to the boat. I dressed as a fisherman, so did my mother. We put the little children in a fish box and covered them with fish. They were told not to move, and not to make a sound. The fish really smelled bad. It almost made them sick. As we left the Saigon Harbor our boat was stopped and boarded. The police looked everywhere. They even jammed a stick into the fish box, but no one moved and we were allowed to continue. After that our trip was long, and we were hungry, but we were not stopped.

The refugee camp in Malaysia was a time for us to learn to wait. Each day we went to the front desk to see if we could begin our new life. Finally, that day came.

Rochester Independent School District 535 initiated the Limited English Proficiency Program (LEP) to aid students. The program had eight objectives. Most focused on English fluency, but the last read, "Retain pride in his/her native culture." Long Ho, a refugee from Vietnam, was employed as a bilingual specialist. "Each day is a new day, a very enriching day," said Ho. "It is a pleasure and an honor to me." Ho translated texts, acted as an interpreter at parent-teacher conferences, and helped troubleshoot discipline problems.

Many youngsters, especially those who were boat people, were tainted, hardened, and old beyond their years. Predictably, these youngsters had adjustment problems. "There was cause for concern last fall and winter when youth scuffles broke out at Mayo and John Marshall high schools and at a local teenage hang out," wrote Greg Sellnow, a *Rochester Post-Bulletin* staff writer. Sellnow told how some Vietnamese traditionally perceived the Cambodians as intellectually inferior. Yet children who had lived under the Pol Pot regime had been deprived of education for years.

Bierbaum described the refugees' experiences at a 1987 mental health workshop for LEP staff members. She said the Southeast Asians were survivors of a holocaust, victims of physical, emotional, sexual, and psychological abuse, who believed "America was heaven." Yet the reality of their situation was that 51.3 percent of the Southeast Asians in Olmsted County were on welfare and 30 to 70 percent experienced mental illness within 10 years. Bierbaum continued, "Someone said recently, 'Our schools wouldn't be so crowded if it weren't for those darned refugees. Why don't they just go back home?' Well, they are home!"

These intense fishermen are participants in the 1987 Rochesterfest Fishing Contest, held at Foster-Arends Park. Prizes were awarded for the largest fish caught, and the most fish caught. Photo by Jerry Olson. Courtesy, Rochester Post-Bulletin

Community groups aided the refugees, among them the Rochester International Association (RIA) and the Intercultural Mutual Assistance Association (IMAA). The RIA was founded in 1981 for the purpose of mutual understanding. "It is believed that this cultural awareness and sharing serves to enrich the fabric of life in the Rochester community and touches the world beyond," explained the RIA brochure. One of the RIA's most famous events is the annual World Festival, which features international displays, foods, arts, crafts, entertainment, and fashions.

The Intercultural Mutual Assistance Association was founded in 1984. "Rochester's IMAA is multi-ethnic and willing to aid any refugee resettled in this city," reported Martha Helgerson in a March 17, 1986, *Rochester Post-Bulletin* article. IMAA focuses on refugee self-help. Refugees receive practical information from the IMAA monthly newsletter, which is published in five languages. One newsletter issue told refugees how to register for garden plots, explained the summer youth employment project, and updated refugees on processing permanent resident cards (green cards).

By 1987 the Southeast Asian refugees comprised roughly 4 percent of the Rochester population. They walk a tightrope between two cultures. Explained Sarah Mason in *They Chose Minnesota: A Survey of the State's Ethnic Groups*, the story of the Southeast Asian refugees is an unfinished one. "Like earlier immigrants from Europe, Africa, and the Western Hemisphere, the Asian peoples seem to be following the dual paths of acculturation and retention. Like the earlier immigrants, too, they have formed various organizations to aid their survival in a new environment—an environment that promised them both hardships and rewards."

The Celebration of a City, organized in 1983 for the 125th anniversary of Rochester, promised merriment. The theme of the celebration was Rochester history. Street names were returned to their origi-

nal names by posting overlays on existing signs. A period fashion show was held, as were historical bus tours, tours of Mayowood, and ongoing entertainment. Six entertainment locations in the downtown area featured 235 separate performances by representatives of the various ethnic groups which had settled Rochester.

Since this type of celebration had never been held before, some worried about the public's response. Financed by the sale of buttons which featured a picture of a goose against the city's skyline, Celebration of a City proved to be a financial and public relations success. The event was renamed Rochesterfest in 1984. As an interesting aside, Mayor Hazama donated leftover "goose" buttons to members of a Mayo Clinic tour group to be used as tokens of friendship. "It was really an experience to walk along a dusty road in China and see kids wearing Rochesterfest buttons!" exclaimed one tour member.

The city's changing skyline became a three-dimensional graph of economic expansion. During the 1980s many new ethnic restaurants—Mexican, Vietnamese, Japanese, and Chinese—opened in Rochester. Louis Letsos and his wife, Rita, opened a small Greek restaurant in 1987. Originally from Delphi, Greece, the couple found Rochester to be the realization of an American dream. Letsos cooked authentic Greek food in an open kitchen so he could interact with his customers. Business proved to be so good that within a year, Letsos was talking about expansion. "I've worked hard," said Letsos. "I'm happy here."

Rochester's building boom mirrored the boom of 1910, which also followed a period of inactivity. Then, as now, new stores and houses were built and existing structures were renovated. The cost of these combined construction projects was estimated at $500,000. "The year has been a banner one in many respects for the future," reported the *Olmsted County Democrat* on July 1, 1910. "Rochester is most assuredly on the map permanently."

"Today" show weatherman Willard Scott broadcasts live from Rochester during Rochesterfest 1987. Willard stands beside Chuck Hazama, probably the only Hawaiian mayor of a midwestern city. Courtesy, Rochester Post-Bulletin

Rochester is definitely on the map. The Rochester Convention and Visitors Bureau estimated that 656,189 people stayed overnight in Rochester during 1987. That same year approximately 830,000 tourists spent an average of $100 a day here, an injection of $83 million into the local economy. In the summer of 1988 Rochester's unemployment rate dropped to 2.3 percent, the lowest in the state. "The 80s have been our decade of progress, but we can look forward to an even more exciting 90s if we commit ourselves in behalf of our city," said Mayor Hazama.

The mayor and his committee were committed to gaining national recognition for Rochester. After three unsuccessful attempts, Rochester received the All-America City award in 1988. A total of 94 cities submitted applications to the National Civic League, but only 10 were selected. Rochester's campaign focused upon human issues, the Greater Rochester Area University Center proposal, the Domestic Abuse Intervention Program, and the Intercultural Mutual Assistance Program.

What makes Rochester unique? It is hard to define the spirit of the city. Visitors have commented about the beauty of Rochester and kindness of its people. Residents have commented about the work ethic and "we can do it" attitude. At age 92, Hilda Wood reminisced about her life here. Asked why she liked Rochester, Wood smiled and said with a slight Norwegian accent, "It isn't too big. It isn't too small. And I always liked my neighbors."

The May 8, 1896, edition of
the Rochester Daily Post
reported that one-half dozen
youngsters were out circulat-
ing the Post among its
"constantly growing list of
subscribers." The newspaper
boys, from left to right, are:
Clarence Sisson, Harry Gil-
man, Irvin Churchill, Ed-
ward Britzius, Arthur Bor-
gart, and Eddie Enquest.
Courtesy, Olmsted County
Historical Society

8

PARTNERS IN PROGRESS

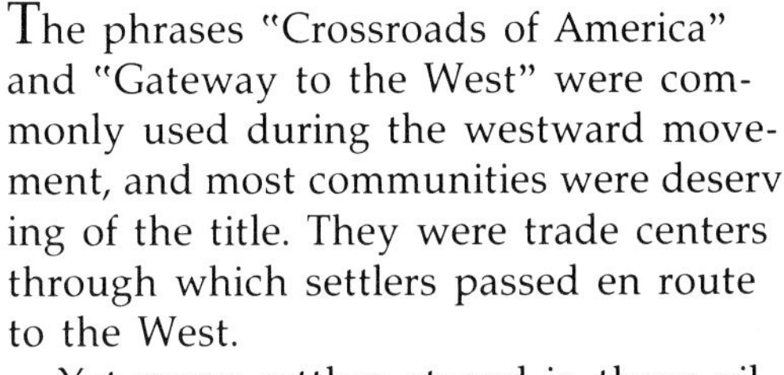

The phrases "Crossroads of America" and "Gateway to the West" were commonly used during the westward movement, and most communities were deserving of the title. They were trade centers through which settlers passed en route to the West.

Yet many settlers stayed in those villages and towns and became vital, creative citizens. Rochester was no different. Some travelers moved on while others remained.

Even during the 1850s Rochester was a crossroad, and it still is today. The old Dubuque Trail entered town from the south, en route to Minneapolis and St. Paul. Other immigrants and pioneers came up the Mississippi River, disembarked at Winona, passed through Rochester, and continued their westward journey. These east-west and north-south crossroads laid the foundation for future trade, transportation, industry, education, and the arts.

Certainly the rolling, wooded hills, pleasant valleys, rivers and streams, and rich farmland provided an attractive diversity to the influx of settlers traveling west.

Rochester was approximately 10 years old when Dr. William Worrall Mayo arrived for his Civil War duties; his arrival marked a turning point for the area's future. One might consider, though, that he may not have wished to remain had the growing community, its businesses, its people, and its potential not been appealing.

Since then others have found this same invitation to stay, work, and enjoy what the Rochester area has to offer. Even today people come from all corners of the world to join those whose roots were established during the city's early years.

Rochester's strategic location—close to interstate highways, its proximity to the Twin Cities, and the nearness of the majestic and scenic bluffs of the Mississippi—have helped to make the city a medical mecca; a prime location for major retail centers, financial institutions, "clean" manufacturing plants, and corporate offices; and a cultural center for the arts.

Few cities of Rochester's size can boast a populace of such high-technology skill—from medical and research science to the engineering skills of large international corporations. While these may have put Rochester on the map, the diverse day-to-day creativity, leadership, and marketing skills of numerous businesses have had their impact on the local economy and ambience of the city.

While each individual, organization, and business has a story to tell, the community itself supported them and gave them opportunities to strive to achieve. Such communities do not just happen; they are created by all people who achieve in their own right by being community organizers and leaders and by working together with purposeful goals.

With its international flavor, impact, and influence on the world, Rochester can be proud of its past, but it is stemming from this very foundation that the area's citizens continue to be "partners in progress."

The organizations whose stories are detailed on the following pages have chosen to support this important literary and civic project. They illustrate the variety of ways in which individuals and their businesses have contributed to Rochester's growth and development.

ROCHESTER AREA CHAMBER OF COMMERCE

Rochester was in its infancy in 1866 when a group was formed to attract more settlers and to protect the rights of farmers bringing wheat to local markets. At that time the Rochester Board of Trade was established with G.W. Van Dunsen as its first president.

From that beginning the board of trade made its presence known, and as the years passed it continued to grow, both in numbers and in the scope of its forthcoming challenges. Changing its name to the Rochester Commercial Club in 1900, its 40 members elected W.L. Breckenridge president, and by the end of the decade the Rochester Commercial Club had incorporated.

In its lengthy statement of purpose, the organization's realm broadened considerably, not only to protect the area's trade but also to advance commercial and manufacturing interests; to promote pleasure, literary, and social culture; to establish commercial, business, and trade relations; and to promote the city.

In 1914 this group raised funds to purchase the 212 First Avenue Southwest building, which housed the organization until 1986, when it moved to its present location at 220 South Broadway in the Holiday Inn Downtown. During the 72 years spent in the original building next to city hall, the organization was renamed the Civic and Commercial Association in 1921, and 10 years later became the Rochester Chamber of Commerce.

As Rochester grew in its post-World War II years, so did its commerce, cultural and leisure scene, economic and business interests, and its needs. To cooperatively address its broadened spectrum of goals and priorities for the city and surrounding area, the group once again changed its name and became the Rochester Area Chamber

The 1984-1985 chamber president Rick Colvin nails up a for-sale sign on the building the Rochester chamber had occupied since 1914. Executive vice-president Mark Ricker and Rochester Convention and Visitors Bureau director Bob Kittley steady the ladder. The chamber moved into new offices at the Holiday Inn Downtown in 1986.

of Commerce in 1968.

Looking at the chamber's achievements over the past decade, it has been instrumental in flood-control legislation, planning the new 7,000-seat Mayo Civic Center with the Park and Recreation Department, and spearheading Rochesterfest events. The chamber also gave birth to the year-and-a-half FutureScan 2000 community strategic planning effort in 1985, initiated the 2+2 concept between Rochester Community College and Winona State University-Rochester Center, and continues to work diligently for downtown redevelopment. In 1986 the chamber brought Rochester Area Economic Development, Inc. (RAEDI), the Service Corps of Retired Executives (SCORE), the Small Business Devel-

opment Center, and the Rochester Convention and Visitors Bureau into its new location as a one-stop business service center.

Ambitious in their efforts, the approximately 950 members of the Rochester Area Chamber of Commerce are proud of the leadership, economic development, legislative, and community growth activities and projects their organization's committee system tackles each year for the betterment of the community.

ALVIN E. BENIKE CONSTRUCTION, INC.

The history of Alvin E. Benike Construction, Inc., which celebrated its 50th anniversary in 1987, is more than a story of steel beams and hard hats. It is also the story of a Rochester family.

Alvin E. Benike, who had been a Rochester carpenter for many years, began his contracting business in his home near St. Mary's Hospital in 1937 with his first commercial project being a butcher shop at the corner of highways 14 and

Alvin E. Benike's construction crew, in 1937, stand in front of the Coca-Cola building site (later the KTTC-TV studio). Benike is at the far right in the top row.

Three generations later Jim, John, and Mary Benike (front row, center) stand with their 1988 construction crew.

52 where Crossroads Shopping Center is now located.

Eldest son Walter, a civil engineer, joined his parents in their establishment in 1948, and their younger son Don, a bricklayer, entered the family enterprise in the mid-1950s.

Walter's children, Jim, John, and Mary, are now at the helm. The last of the slide rule generation, Jim began to work for the company in 1972 upon graduation from Iowa State University as a construction engineer. In 1978 John paralleled his brother's education and joined the firm. Mary followed both of her brothers' footsteps and came into the business in 1987.

Employing an average of 80 people year round and as many as 150 during peak times, Jim credits Benike's growth in recent years to the leadership of many of its key employees who have served the company for 30 years or more.

Numerous projects dot the city and surrounding area, establishing an impressive portfolio: the Alfred Research Building of St. Marys, the Harwick Building, schools, restaurants, churches, condominiums, and office buildings.

Pleased to be part of Rochester's plan for building a better future, the firm's current projects include work on the D-5 Office Plaza Building, the Mayo Education Building, Mayo North, and the Radisson Hotel. During this peak construction period a tremendous accomplishment was achieved when 60 workers poured 485 yards of concrete in a matter of hours at the Radisson site.

Even with many large-scale projects under way, Jim is quick to point out, "We are in the service business, not just the construction business. We value our repeat customers, and we want to be of service to them in any way that we can. Customer satisfaction is our goal."

Just like their grandfather and father before them, Jim, John, and Mary believe that serving their community is very important. Jim is on the Rochester Area Chamber of Commerce Board of Directors, a past officer of the YMCA and a past member on its board of directors, a past president of the Rochester Area Builders Association, and is active in numerous other professional and service organizations.

In addition to being a member of many of the same organizations as Jim, John recently served as fundraising chairman of the Minnesota Private College Association.

Alvin E. Benike Construction, Inc., is proud of its legacy of service to the community for the past half-century and looks forward to serving in the future.

WEIS COMPANIES

At the turn of the century a young man in Trintering, Luxembourg, began his apprenticeship as a cabinetmaker. Working beside a master craftsman, he learned not only woodworking skills but also the patience and pride that give meaning to the words "old-world craftsmanship."

Had he stayed in his village, he—and his sons after him—may have remained simple cabinetmakers. But the winds of change drove the young man, John Weis, to southeastern Minnesota. At first he worked as a farmhand and railroad laborer. But after two years of service in World War I, Weis returned to his craft.

For 20 years he was employed by others. But in 1939 he started a cabinet shop in the basement of his home near Silver Lake. As the quality of his workmanship became more widely known, customers began asking his help with remodeling work. Word soon spread to the business community. Before long Weis and his two employees had gone far beyond cabinetmaking. The company that became

John Weis, founder of Weis Builders, Inc.

known as Weis Builders, Inc., soon was one of the largest residential and commercial contractors in southern Minnesota.

Weis' sons, Eugene and Joseph, worked with their father, learning his carpentry and business skills. Eugene joined the firm in 1946 upon returning from military service. Joe soon followed after studying architectural drafting and estimating at Dunwoody Industrial Institute in Minneapolis.

When John Weis died in 1952, Eugene and Joe carried on the family tradition. Their first independent job was modest: building a simple garage. For a time they continued to be primarily residential and commercial remodelers. But as their father's skill and ambition had carried him beyond cabinetmaking, the sons' brought them to the threshold of larger things. They began constructing commercial and light industrial buildings. The first of these was the Knights of Columbus Hall, which still stands on Rochester's Beltline.

In 1960 they incorporated under the name Weis Builders, Inc.

Joe Weis served as president and general manager, handling project bidding and overall management of the company. Eugene, as vice-president, supervised the construction of all projects.

Until 1970 Weis had always built for others. Now the firm became a developer in its own right, developing and constructing government-assisted housing. The first such project in Rochester was the 104-unit Rochester Square Apartments.

Over the next 10 years Weis developed and built 23 projects consisting of 1,100 units in 17 communities located in three states.

When the government-assisted housing market declined, the organization concentrated on building and developing shopping centers and lease-back buildings, while continuing to maintain its position in the competitive bid market. Since 1983 Weis has been codeveloper and has built 19 centers consisting of 1.7 million square feet of space.

Still another concept the Weis or-

Eugene and Joseph Weis in the late 1950s. Under their leadership the company experienced dramatic growth.

Wies Companies' home office in northwest Rochester.

Joe Weis is currently a director of the National Association of Home Companies, is on the board of directors of the Companies Association of Minnesota, is past president of the Minnesota Multi-Housing Association, past president of the Minnesota Associated General Contractors, past president of the Rochester Area Chamber of Com-

ganization employs is the design/build method of construction. Design/build is a one-source responsibility method that finds Weis Companies assisting a client by locating a site, purchasing it, designing the building, securing all permits, and dealing with all boards, governmental agencies, and subcontractors. Management selects an individual project manager who coordinates all aspects of the project, and a project superintendent who assists him by supervising the six construction-related trades employed by Weis Companies.

Another innovative step toward diversification was taken in 1971 when David Busch joined the brothers in establishing Weis Management Corporation. Managing properties the firm developed and built, as well as managing property for other owners, became the next arena in the operation. Managing more than 50 properties in the tristate area of Minnesota, Wisconsin, and Iowa, the company's clients include individuals, partnerships, corporations, and nonprofit organizations.

Under Busch's leadership and expertise, Weis Management Corporation is one of only 506 firms in the United States that has earned the coveted Accredited Management Organization (AMO) designation from the Institute of Real Es-

The 1989 board of directors of Weis Builders, Inc., are (seated, from left) Larry L. Corbin, president; Joseph C. Weis, chairman of the board; Ruth M. Jensen, secretary/treasurer; and Erik J. Weis. Standing (from left) are Ronald D. Kreinbring, senior vice-president; and Jay B. Weis.

tate Management. This designation is the hallmark of professionalism in real estate property management.

John Weis; his sons, Eugene (now deceased) and Joe; and his two grandsons, Erik and Jay, continue to leave their mark on Rochester. Looking at Weis Companies' brief, one sees a lengthy list of projects that include local and area seniors' residences, luxury condominiums, schools, churches, shopping centers, restaurants, and office buildings. If one were to count each project, the list totals more than 450 buildings throughout the tristate area.

Community, church, and trade affiliations read like the long list of Weis projects. Active in the Rochester Area Chamber of Commerce, the Independent Republican Party, and various trade organizations,

merce, and will serve as president of Companies Association of Minnesota in 1990.

The company celebrated its 50th year in business during 1989. These years have seen phenomenal growth and change, but three things have remained the same: Weis quality craftsmanship, a commitment to the local community, and family tradition. Jay and Erik Weis, third-generation members of the Weis family, are already helping prepare Weis Companies to be Rochester's builder of the twenty-first century.

THE JOHNSON COMPANY

Clifford M. Johnson, founder of the firm that bears his name, came to Rochester in 1953 as an AB Dick duplicating equipment and supplies distributor. Now, after more than 35 years, few people could duplicate Johnson's community leadership and dedication.

When he started his sales and service business for southern Minnesota, Johnson and his two employees—his wife, Evelyn, and associate Donald Butters—shared office space with another firm at the corner of 102 East Center Street. Three years later the firm moved their business to larger quarters at 511 First Avenue Southwest.

In 1958, a few years after AB Dick introduced its first offset press, the firm decided to expand the enterprise to include commercial printing in order to better serve its customers. Starting with letterheads, stationery, and other business-related, small print jobs, the operation has continued to keep pace with the rapidly changing world of printing.

Opening branch offices in Mason City, Iowa, and Mankato in the mid-1970s, the firm continued to expand in Rochester with the purchase of the former Whiting Press Printing Company at 311 Second Avenue Northwest in 1980. Among the four sites, 95 employees are presently engaged in all phases of the full-service printing company and sales organization.

Rochester's southwest site continues to be the sales and service center for the firm's AB Dick offices. Since 1987 the print shop for both small and large jobs is located at the northwest site.

Clifford Johnson left his mark on the business community as an entrepreneur. The results of his stalwart belief that individuals and businesses must "pay their dues" to

Clifford M. Johnson, owner and chairman of the board of the Johnson Company, recognizes the importance of serving his community as well as servicing his customers.

the community in return for its support is perhaps his greatest legacy to Rochester. His list of achievements reads like the yellow pages, for his dedication is unceasing. Not only was he president of the Chamber of Commerce Downtown Council, but he also has served as president of United Way, the YMCA, and Kiwanis; chairman of Rochester Methodist Hospital Foundation, Rochester Art Center, and state chairman of the Red Cross Fund; and board member of Rochester Foundation, Salvation Army, and Rochester Civic Music, to name only a few of his endeavors.

Johnson was the first Rochester businessperson to be inducted into Minnesota's Business Hall of Fame (1979), was recipient of the Rochester Mayor's Medal of Honor, and received the Sertoma's Service to Mankind Award. He has also excelled professionally: Johnson was named Outstanding AB Dick Distributor five times.

Now retired, though still chairman of the board at the Johnson Company, Clifford is pleased that his daughter and two sons are continuing the family's tradition of quality printing and equipment sales. Likewise, Don Butters, president of the Johnson Company, shares his deep respect for Cliff Johnson's professional and community ideals by instilling those principles in all Johnson employees.

IBM ROCHESTER

Today IBM Rochester is the mid-range commercial computer systems capital of the world, manufacturing high-technology data-processing files and systems. It is one of Minnesota's top 10 private-sector employers with approximately 7,000 employees.

Since February 8, 1956, when IBM announced that it would build an $8-million plant in Rochester, overwhelming expansion has taken place. IBM president Thomas J. Watson, Jr., said the new plant, to be constructed on 397 acres of farmland in northwest Rochester, would be completed and in operation the following year and would employ 1,500 people by 1958.

The facility's initial 400,000 square feet, housing manufacturing, engineering, and education, has now increased to 3.5 million square feet on 586 acres. With 32 buildings, it is the largest IBM facility under one contiguous roof in the world.

On May 10, 1956, IBM opened temporary management headquarters in downtown Rochester with four key people. Construction had begun for leased manufacturing facilities on the Industrial Opportunity, Inc., site, where Ability Building Center is presently located.

IBM employees began working at IOI's building on August 27, 1956. Manufacturing activity started immediately on IBM's 077 Numeric Collator, with the first machine shipped just two days after the plant opened.

It was on March 15, 1957, that occupancy began at the new, permanent site, and since then IBM Rochester has continued to expand its product line, space needs, and number of employees.

Under corporate-wide reorganization in 1988, IBM Rochester became the principal site for IBM Application Business Systems. This organization is responsible for worldwide product development, including product line revenue, profit growth, return on assets, and marketing planning, as well as U.S. manufacturing for IBM midrange system products, intermediate and low-end storage devices, and operating systems software.

A June 1988 announcement by site general manager Larry Osterwise gave the industry assurance of IBM's continued impact in the mid-range computer marketplace. IBM Rochester's unveiling of its new AS/400 computer system was heralded as the biggest product announcement ever. It characterizes the firm's pursuit of product excellence while serving its customers' needs.

Adhering to Watson's belief that, "We all owe a duty to the community in which we live and to society at large," IBM Rochester's charitable contributions and community involvement also have tremendous impact. Its computer lit-

Pictured here is a view of the entrance to IBM Rochester.

eracy program, Teach the Teachers, has trained more than 10,000 junior and senior high school teachers and students throughout Minnesota.

Another major IBM community effort is sharing its expertise in effective people and resource management with community and nonprofit leaders through its Community Services Management Seminars.

IBM Rochester's contributions to culture and the arts, to health and human services, as well as to numerous civic and community activity organizations are far-reaching through financial support and donation of its equipment and products.

IBM Rochester's employees and visitors are greeted by attractively landscaped entrances and courtyards.

SCHMIDT PRINTING INC.

Few people reading magazines and trade journals realize that many insert cards offering subscriptions and other information are made at Rochester's Schmidt Printing, Inc.

More than 10 million cards, requiring more than 50 tons of paper, are printed each day at the organization's 1416 Valley High Drive Northwest plant. Schmidt insert cards appear in more than 300 consumer magazines and trade journals nationwide.

A former pressman, Gustave Schmidt, the company's founder, bought a press and in 1912 located his fledgling business above a South Broadway grocery store. Six years later he constructed a building at 19 North Broadway to house both his printing firm and a hotel, which he named after his son, Norman. Both establishments occupied the site until 1949, when they moved to 503-507 North Broadway.

After Gustave's death in 1930, his wife, Dorothy, and sons Norman and Harold served the printing needs of Rochester for more than 30 years. Schmidt's calendars, printed from 1963 to 1968 and featuring old photos of the Rochester area, have become collectors' items. Harold's son, Casey, continued the tradition when he purchased the company in 1966. After the facility fell victim to a teenage arsonist the following year, Schmidt Printing moved to its present location in 1968.

After selling the business to Sacred Design, Inc., a Minneapolis-based designer and producer of church bulletins, Casey Schmidt stayed with the company as president and general manager. This sale altered the identity of Schmidt Printing from that of a locally based operation to an in-house supplier for a larger corpora-

An early Schmidt Printing employee, Carl Vaughn, sets type in this photo from one of the firm's notable calendars published in the 1960s.

tion.

Still another sale in 1976 found Sacred Design, Inc., selling the printing firm back to Schmidt and Al Tuntland, a Rochester entrepreneur.

At this point Schmidt Printing began to look for opportunities beyond Rochester. In 1977 the firm opened a sales office in Minneapolis; by 1981 clients from New York, Los Angeles, and Chicago were coming to Schmidt Printing for their business needs.

Al Tuntland became sole owner of the company in 1983; today Schmidt Printing's main product lines, in addition to magazine insert cards, are direct-mail letters, brochures, and catalogs.

Enlarging and remodeling the main plant in 1983 doubled its size. With several expansions since then, the firm now occupies more than 80,000 square feet. From the one-man print shop in 1912, Schmidt Printing, Inc., now runs three shifts five days a week, employing in excess of 200 full- and part-time workers.

Tuntland not only led his company to national recognition as an award-winning industry leader in 1984-1985, but he is also a Rochester civic leader. Tuntland is chairman of FutureScan 2000 (a task force engaged in long-range strategic planning for Olmsted County), is on the chamber of commerce board of directors, and serves on the board of the Minnesota Chamber of Commerce and Industry. He is also on the Regent's Advisory Board for the University of Minnesota in Rochester.

MEPC APACHE PROPERTIES, INC.

Shopping in general is something nearly everyone takes for granted. To the present-day generation, shopping centers are nothing unusual. However, the concept of shopping malls has not been around very long.

Since Southdale in Bloomington—the granddaddy of enclosed shopping centers—opened in 1957, not only has shopping under one roof made its mark on the retail marketing scene, but the concept also has become firmly established in America's family and social life.

Apache Mall in Rochester opened its doors to area shoppers on October 16, 1969, on its 43-acre site in southwest Rochester. Opening with 29 stores, Apache grew to 39 stores in its first three years of operation. In 1972 Dayton's joined the mall. Today, in addition to Dayton's, JCPenney, and Montgomery Ward as anchors, 80 retail shops line the mall's corridors with 21 of the original 29 retailers still in the group.

However, like fashions, retail trends change. One such trend has been for large numbers of smaller

Apache Mall's recent remodeling uses projected, three-dimensional storefronts, large expanses of windows for displays, and new lighting to illuminate shopping corridors.

stores to occupy a mall's large expanse. Thus, in 1981 a major renovation began to make room for additional merchants. The former Red Owl supermarket became a fashion court housing several specialty stores and accessory shops. Similarly, other areas were reconfigured, allowing for more retailers.

With its $1.5-million renovation, completed in 1985, a new look came to the mall. Three-dimensional, pop-out storefronts create a "main street" look granting more individual personality to stores.

Soft colors, mirrored walls, skylighting, and a specially designed tivoli lighting system brighten and enlarge interiors. Designers employed increased interiorscaping, using 20-foot ficus trees, hundreds of smaller plants, and park benches providing a cheery, comfortable atmosphere.

As Apache Mall's marketing director states, "Shopping centers have become the town square. With this type of attractive physical setting, we can establish a good balance between our merchandising events and our community-oriented events. It's our way of giving something back to the community."

During most of the year's 52

weeks, Apache provides a community forum for numerous organizations, all in the confines of its merchandising area of 715,000 square feet.

Sara Jorgensen, Apache Mall's marketing director, and Richard Landwehr, general manager, indicate that Apache Mall's market is well defined; it is a middle market with an extensive regional draw from a seven-county area, with shoppers also coming from northern Iowa and western Wisconsin.

Originally owned by the Apache Corporation of Minneapolis, Apache Mall became the property of MEPC in 1977. MEPC's U.S. headquarters is located in Dallas, Texas. This American investment property company is owned by parent firm, MEPC, plc, of London.

Worldwide, MEPC has a strong portfolio of office and retail properties. While the Dallas corporate offices of MEPC manages investments in Dallas, Las Vegas, Chicago, Minneapolis, and Rochester, the London office manages its other investment properties worldwide.

Shoppers relax in one of Apache Mall's courtyards.

PACE DAIRY FOODS COMPANY, INC.

PACE Dairy Foods' cheese-packaging and labeling operations are conducted from this building at 2700 Valley High Drive Northwest.

PACE Dairy Foods' products reflect today's growing popularity of palate-pleasing cheeses in all their zesty flavors. Chefs garnish their entrees and salads with tasty cheese sauces, and party-goers savor beguiling trays of assorted cheeses on hors d'oeuvre tables.

While PACE Dairy Foods Company, Inc., a wholly owned subsidiary of the Kroger Company, makes its own processed cheese, it is a processor and packager of natural cheeses for other brand-name labels. Packaging for its clients' individual labels, the firm's accounts include major supermarket chains as well as wholesalers and dairy stores nationwide.

When the parent firm became interested in a cheese program back in the late 1960s, its Dairy Foods Division investigated the potential for supplying stores with a complete line of cheese products. Southeastern Minnesota was found to be the ideal location for such a project.

In October 1970, 24,000 square feet of production space was leased from A.M.P.I. in southeast Rochester, and PACE Dairy Foods began the cutting and wrapping of natural cheeses. However, plans were already in motion to construct a facility to expand its natural cheese lines, as well as to enter into the processed cheese market.

In the summer of 1973 the orga-

Sheets of processed cheese are being sliced and layered before the cheese moves on to be packaged and labeled.

nization purchased a 27-acre site on the city's northwest outskirts and construction began. One year later the cutting, wrapping, and labeling operation was transferred to the new facility at 2700 Valley High Drive Northwest, with Harold Miller as the site's first manager. In 1979 additional space was added.

One of the most modern cheese plants in the world, PACE was the first to use many innovative systems. Setting that precedent was PACE's production of an individually wrapped sliced cheese. After developing and installing a system in August 1976, PACE Dairy

Foods had a successful and novel, individually wrapped, sliced cheese operation. This innovation became a major factor in the Rochester plant's success.

Huge blocks of solid, natural cheese are shipped into PACE; in fact, 5 million pounds of bulk

cheese blocks are on hand at any given time. In operations that run 24 hours a day, this bulk cheese is stripped, cleaned, and profiled into various shapes and sizes for customer use—brick, slices, or shredded. The cheese is then wrapped, weighted, and labeled for a customer account, and shipped out again ready for the display shelf.

PACE is autonomous from its parent company and has its own local management team, engineering staff, sales force, personnel and accounting departments, and procurement and distribution operation.

The success of PACE Dairy Foods Company, Inc., can best be summed up by general manager Walt Ehret's statement, "Our ingredient is quality, and our product is pride."

MAYO CLINIC

Mayo Clinic traces its heritage to the practice of frontier doctor William Worrall Mayo, an Englishman who came to America in 1845.

Moving west with his wife, Louise, and their family and settling in LeSeuer, Minnesota, he became the Union Army's examining surgeon for southern Minnesota recruits in 1863, headquartered in Rochester.

Sons William James ("Dr. Will") and Charles Horace ("Dr. Charlie") joined their father's practice in the 1880s, incorporated his idealism, and continued to follow his lead in developing surgical skills.

On August 21, 1883, a tornado struck Rochester, leaving death, destruction, and many injured residents. The elder Dr. Mayo, seeking nursing care for the injured, asked the teaching Sisters of St. Francis for assistance. Using their convent as a temporary hospital gave Mother Alfred the idea of establishing a hospital. Thus began a relationship between the Mayos and St. Mary's Hospital that has lasted more than a century.

Physicians came from around the world to the Mayo's operating rooms to observe and hear the running commentary. These informal classes, known as the Mayo's

Dr. William Worrall Mayo flanked by his sons, Dr. Charlie (left) and Dr. William J. Mayo (right). Photo circa 1890

clinic, helped spread the practice's reputation and also gave the place its name.

As the family practice grew (it later included Dr. Charlie's son, Dr. Chuck, who had his own distinguished Mayo career), the Mayos invited other doctors into partnership, which later became the nonprofit Mayo Foundation. The Mayos' organization initiated a new idea in American medicine—the multispecialty group practice.

Patients liked this new practice. In 1907, with eight staff members, 5,000 patients registered; by 1912, 15,000 registered; and two years later that figure doubled to 30,000 patients registering with 17 permanent staff members.

Today there are 864 staff physicians and medical scientists and 15,162 total employees in Rochester at Mayo, St. Mary's Hospital, and Rochester Methodist Hospital, with approximately 283,000 patients registered in 1987. More than 4 million persons, from all 50 states and more than 150 foreign countries, have been Mayo patients since 1907.

Research and education have had emphasis since the early days. Numerous discoveries dot Mayo Clinic history. In 1933 the nation's first blood bank was established at Mayo. In 1950 Drs. Edward Kendall and Philip Hench received the Nobel Prize for discovering cortisone. Discovery of thyroxin, the development of nonsurgical treatment for gallstones, and advances in tuberculosis treatment, chemotherapy, and open-heart surgery are other milestones.

In 1915 the Mayo Graduate School of Medicine, the first of its kind, was established and has trained more than 10,000 alumni who practice, teach, and do research worldwide. Today it has the largest graduate medical education program in the world. Mayo Medical School and the School of Health-Related Sciences augment the education objective.

In 1986 Mayo Clinic, St. Mary's Hospital, and Rochester Methodist Hospital integrated under governance of Mayo Foundation. New Mayo clinics opened in Jacksonville, Florida, in 1986 and Scottsdale, Arizona, in 1987.

The Mayo Foundation campus in downtown Rochester is dominated by the Mayo Building to the left and the Plummer Building (center). In 1987 construction began on a new education building and Mayo North, adjacent to Rochester Methodist Hospital. Construction to add on to the Guggenheim Building (right) and the Hilton Building was also begun.

MADONNA TOWERS, INC.

It began, as so many successful projects have, because there was a definite need for the burgeoning population of retirement-age citizens. With 5,000 people joining the ranks of the elderly daily in our nation, innovative and sensible programs have become imperative.

Owned and operated by the Missionary Oblates of Mary Immaculate, Central U.S. Province, St. Paul, Madonna Towers' futuristic plan became a pioneering model. When ground was broken at its May 26, 1965, ceremony, this plan became a reality. Twelve acres of land were attractively transformed into a 14-story complex offering both independent living and continuing care.

When Madonna Towers, Inc., opened its doors in Rochester in January 1967, the concept of a retirement community with continuing care was in its infancy. Now, 20 years later, other facilities are employing this philosophy, which offers residents freedom, security,

Madonna Towers, an innovative community for the elderly, features resident town homes and apartments and a 14-story complex that houses a dining room, nursing care, and administrative services.

mobility, recreation, and service for their retirement years, and, when necessary, short- or long-term nursing care.

Especially designed for retirement living, Madonna Towers' apartments and town homes offer a choice of quality, private residences. Today, with 139 apartments, 9 town houses, and a 62-bed skilled-nursing facility, residents enjoy their new homes located within a typical residential neighborhood of single-family dwellings and apartments.

Every aspect of a person's life is considered—social, educational, cultural, spiritual, and physical. Active retirees nurture their favorite roses, vegetables, and herbs in their gardens on the beautifully landscaped acreage. Having tea with visitors in the gazebo or in one of the pleasant courtyards is also a favorite pastime.

In addition, staff activity directors arrange schedules, transportation, and ticket purchases for a variety of concerts, plays, sporting events, and shopping excursions for those who wish to participate. Still others attend such events without taking advantage of such plan-

Reverend William Coovert, OMI, speaks at the Madonna Towers' ground-breaking ceremonies on May 26, 1965.

ning.

"That's the beauty of this concept," says Alice McHale, director. "Residents can be as independent as they wish to be, be active only in a very limited manner, or be completely involved."

While Madonna Towers is governed by the Missionary Oblates, it is ecumenical in every respect. With its own attractive chapel, solitude and opportunity for spiritual enrichment are available to members of all faiths. Moreover, pastors from the city's numerous churches visit regularly and participate in many of the activities.

The project celebrated its 20th anniversary in 1987. It saw expansion from its opening days. Madonna Towers reached its residence capacity in 1972, enlarged its skilled nursing care facility from the initial 24 beds to its present 62 beds, saw its staff enlarge to 137 employees, and recently completed exterior improvements.

One thing has not changed, however, and that is its hospitality and caring concern for the elderly. Perhaps, too, having had directors such as Father Al Henger for 15 years, as well as Duane Pidcock, Steve Wuitschick, and Alice McHale, its continuity of stable administration contributes greatly to the satisfaction of Madonna Towers' community of elders.

CLEMENTS CHEVROLET-CADILLAC-SUBARU COMPANY

Few business establishments can boast of a history spanning six decades. Fewer still have passed the ownership of that business down three generations through sons-in-law.

Unusual as this may be, the Clements Chevrolet-Cadillac-Subaru dealership has done just that. In business in Rochester for 66 years, it also holds the distinction of being the oldest, continuously family-owned automobile dealership in Rochester. Clements' Mankato automobile dealership got its start 75

F. Braden Clements founded Clements Chevrolet.

years ago, just two years after Louis Chevrolet's first Chevrolet automobile was produced in 1911.

Braden Clements began his Rochester Chevrolet dealership in 1922. Purchasing the Case Building on the 300 block of First Avenue Southwest, Clements continued at that location until the early 1950s, when the dealership relocated just one block south, also on First Avenue Southwest.

James Madden, Braden Clements' son-in-law, became the Chevrolet dealer in 1952. Braden Clements died in 1969. That same year James Madden decided to move the dealership from the down-

town area and purchased a tract of land on the south side of highways 14 and 52. Relocating from the downtown business district was a bold move, but it was not long before other retailers followed Clements to the adjacent, newly opened Apache Mall. Soon other auto dealerships followed the trend, moving from downtown to outlying areas.

In 1984 Madden's son-in-law, Jerry Bridwell, became the dealer at Clements Chevrolet.

While the old locations could display only three cars in the showroom, the present facility can display approximately 15 vehicles. With close to $10 million worth of cars on the lot at any given time, Clements is one of the largest, non-metropolitan dealerships in Minnesota. Moreover, as a full-line dealership, its 91 employees are working within a system composed of five separate businesses, including a new car business, a used car business, a parts business, a service business, and a body shop.

As is similar to other retail oper-

ations, trends change. Today women are major decision-makers in more than 50 percent of automobile sales. Dealerships also seek female sales associates with the right skills to serve the automobile market. Other trends, changes, and challenges in the auto industry are smaller cars with more efficient engines (primarily due to government-mandated fleet mileage requirements). Yet to come will be cars with high-tech computerized functions.

Bridwell notes the highly visible and convenient location of Clements Chevrolet-Cadillac-Subaru Company at Highway 14 and Apache Mall as one factor that sets his establishment apart from other automobile dealerships. Another component is its business policy of taking care of present customers as well as seeking new ones.

However, Bridwell reflects on the 66-year track record, indicative of the kind of sales and service the firm provides, as the real key to this dealership's success. Such longevity says a great deal for any business.

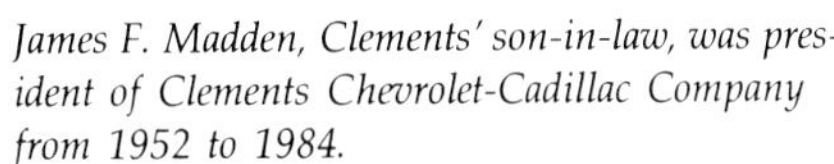

James F. Madden, Clements' son-in-law, was president of Clements Chevrolet-Cadillac Company from 1952 to 1984.

Gerald A. Bridwell, Madden's son-in-law, is the current president of Clements Chevrolet-Cadillac-Subaru Company.

BARLOW FOODS, INC.

While Neil Armstrong and Buzz Aldrin made history walking on the moon in July 1969, Rochester made its own history on July 27, 1969, when Stephen B. Barlow held his Rochester supermarket's grand opening on a Sunday. Prior to that day, no local supermarkets had ever been open on Sundays. Controversial as this was, two other supermarkets followed his example the next week and opened their doors to Sunday shoppers. Since then, Sunday shopping has become a common practice.

Barlow came to Rochester from Minneapolis, where he built his first supermarket in suburban Crystal in 1957. Knowing the kind of store he wanted—one with top-quality foods, upscale decor, and no price advertising or sales gimmicks—Barlow took market surveys, and they indicated that Rochester would be a prime location.

Other firsts followed as soon as Barlow Foods opened. Ideas new to the supermarket scene included having a registered dietician and/or home economist, an un-

Barlow shoppers select fresh flowers, foliage plants, or floral arrangements at their international flower market. Photo circa 1969

derground conveyor for parcel pickup, a restaurant, a delicatessen, and state-of-the-art computer capability.

His innovative enterprise was true to its theme of an international marketplace with ethnic and gourmet selections in addition to quality foods. Upscale decor with carpeted floors, decorative wall coverings, a floral market, and international flags was symbolic of the coat-of-arms logo that became the enterprise's distinctive trademark.

Approximately 10,000 people crowded into the new facility's 25,000 square feet at 1315 Sixth Street Northwest that first day, and they have been coming every day since then. Today Barlow Foods has the highest daily customer count of any supermarket in the state of Minnesota.

Its pledge to bring the customer the best variety of top-quality food with the finest service and convenience at the lowest-possible prices became the store's marketing philosophy. Barlow blends the most up-to-date food-merchandising techniques and still

maintains the old-fashioned, personalized, grocery store tradition. These basics continue to be stressed to employees today.

As pursuit of these goals brought high customer volume, expansions became necessary. In 1975 there was an addition of 15,000 square feet, and when the shopping plaza was built in 1982, another 12,000 square feet were added, bringing the supermarket to its present 52,000 square feet. Employment increased, too, from 90 people in 1969, to the current 310 for its 168-hour week.

Carrying on the tradition of excellence established by their maternal grandfather, Robert E. Weber, a longtime Minneapolis grocer, and their father, Stephen B., is today's third generation: Stephen R., chief financial officer, and sisters Cathy Mestad and Bonnie Mitchell.

Active on various committees in the community, Stephen B. also served as president of the National Grocers Association. Stephen R. is on the Minnesota State Chamber of Commerce board and has participated on several community, political, and trade association committees. Bonnie and Cathy play major roles in Barlow Foods, Inc., and are also involved in community projects.

Stephen B. Barlow hosts the gala July 27, 1969, grand opening of Barlow Foods, Inc. As suggested by the elegant table setting, the upscale supermarket features top-quality foods as shown in this picture of a Barlow produce department.

FIKSDAL FLOWERS

Long before the advertising slogan, "Say it with flowers," became popular, Fiksdal Flowers was doing just that.

Ed Fiksdal came to Rochester in the late 1930s as a flower shop employee, and in 1947 brother Mads, a San Francisco flower shop veteran, and another brother, Aldin, joined him.

Buying a house at 1227 Second Street Southwest, across from St. Mary's Hospital, the three brothers built onto the front and side of the house for their shop. Though scoffed at for moving from the downtown shopping area, they opened their establishment on October 18, 1947, and were the only employees. Space was later added to the back of the shop, and in 1975 the first floor and basement of the house became office and work space. Joining FTD in the late 1940s, the business has grown continuously and now employs 12 people.

Though Aldin dropped out of the partnership in 1950 and Ed became sole owner in 1987, it continues to be the oldest business in the area owned and operated by the same proprietorship. The Fiksdal children worked while youngsters, and currently Ed's son, Gary, is shop manager, and daughter Nancy is office manager. While Ed claims to be retired, he still comes to the shop daily.

Pleased that his flowers bring joy to all recipients, he claims that weddings are the most gratifying. Ed still plans with the bride, personally pins on corsages, gives last-minute touches to floral arrangements, and extends his congratulations.

Second Street Southwest's commercial strip across from St. Mary's Hospital was strictly a residential street when the Fiksdal brothers bought this house in 1947 for their floral shop.

EXPRESS SERVICES, TEMPORARY AND PERMANENT PERSONNEL, AND ROBERT WILLIAM JAMES & ASSOCIATES

Believing that a company's success or failure is directly related to the quality of its personnel, Mark and Sheryl Tasler, owners of Express Services, Temporary and Permanent Personnel, and Robert William James & Associates, have directed their 14 years in Rochester toward successfully matching thousands of needs of client employers to skills of applicants.

Their Express franchise is a three-fold operation. Among the fastest growing industries in the nation today, Express Temporary daily provides hundreds of employees to Rochester area businesses. The permanent placement division recruits and places quality candidates in mid-level business support positions, while RWJ & Associates provides technical and upper-level management recruiting services to local and national clients. As a full-service employment center, the staff of 15 professionals conducts comprehensive reviews of all employee candidates on behalf of their clients.

A vision, a dream, determination, and a commitment to excellence saw the business expand from its first 450-square-foot office at Northgate Shopping Center in 1974 to its new office building and present location at 2360 North Broadway.

Offering all three employment services under one roof is unique, and the Taslers' success was recognized with Express' Professionalism Award in 1987 and 1988. Locally they were honored with the Rochester Area Chamber of Commerce's Small Business Award in 1987.

Mark is a regional developer

Mark and Sheryl Tasler, owners of Express Services, Temporary and Permanent Personnel, and Robert William James & Associates.

for Express Franchises in Minnesota and neighboring states. Both Taslers are active chamber of commerce committee members, its Ambassadors and Diplomats, United Way, Sertoma, Toastmasters, Rotary, and numerous other civic, school, and church organizations.

K&K REALTY OF ROCHESTER, INC.

For the past 50 years the owners of K&K Realty have been pacesetters in the real estate business.

In the 1940s, when few women were in the business, Katherine Kilbourne began her real estate career; but it was not until she and Eleanor Kirklin became partners that K&K Realty was established. Since that time women have played major roles in the firm, and in the local, state, and national real estate scene.

Each partnership from that point on set precedents that encouraged sales associates and others in real estate to pursue excellence. Throughout the years Kilbourne, Kirklin, Peg Place, Dorothy Wood, Enid Baker, and today's partnership of Marilyn Stewart and Deborah Dison have emphasized professionalism, education, and community involvement.

Achievements dot each ownership. Kirklin was the first female president for Rochester's Board of REALTORS, with Peg Place becoming the second woman to hold the title. Of the five women who have held the post, K&K boasts three, in 1986 Marilyn Stewart became its third female president.

Statewide, too, K&K has been recognized. Place was the first Minnesota woman to earn the Certified Residential Broker designation, and in 1974 she directed Minnesota's real estate education. Stewart's educational leadership saw her become education chairman for both Rochester's and Minnesota's Association of REALTORS. In 1989 Stewart became the first female president of this 12,000-member association.

Owing to its professional real estate education emphasis, K&K is the only Rochester company whose entire staff holds the GRI designation, a requirement by the firm. It also has the highest percentage of CRS (Certified Residential Specialists) designated REALTORS in Minnesota.

Taking their endeavors to the national level, Place was national president of the Women's Council of REALTORS, and Stewart holds the distinction of being the first Minnesota woman named to the National Board of REALTORS' Board of Directors, in addition to being the first Minnesotan on the national CRB Council.

Dison directs her efforts toward the relocation service net-

Pictured here are Deborah Dison (seated), CRB, CRS, vice-president and broker-owner of K&K Realty; Marilyn D. Stewart (standing left), CRB, CRS, president and principal broker-owner; and Eleanor J. Kirklin, surviving founder of K&K Realty.

work, serving communities nationwide and worldwide, as well as local and state grievance committees.

At the outset, with limited First National Bank Building office space, Rochester's Multiple Listing Service was also begun and maintained by K&K for several years. Wood and Baker moved it to its present location at 607 Second Street Southwest in 1976. The firm now has 20 sales associates and three office staff members.

Through the years each woman brought her talents, business acumen, and organizational skills to define the company's expectations. Perhaps most noticeable locally, however, is their advertising concept, using pen-and-ink drawings of homes for sale, indicative of innovative marketing skills.

A recent comment best illustrates their dedication: "I can remember when people all over town said, 'Those girls will never make it in business,' and now look at what you have done."

An artist's rendering of the K&K Realty office.

KTTC-TV & KROC RADIO

Rochester owes both its radio and television broadcast services to the perseverance of Gregory Gentling, former publisher and editor of two Rochester newspapers, the *Post* and the *Morning Journal.*

When Twin Cities' newspaper, radio, and television crewmen came to Rochester to cover President Franklin D. Roosevelt's appearance honoring Drs. William and Charles Mayo on August 4, 1934, Gentling saw potential for a local radio station.

His contacts with that media's personnel laid the groundwork for establishing the Southern Minnesota Broadcasting Company in 1935. Station KROC-AM went on the air September 30, 1935, from its first studio located in the Martin Hotel.

On the air for approximately 18 hours a day, KROC was first at 1310 on the radio dial, but due to FCC changes, the station later went to 1340, where it remains today. KROC-FM began in July 1965.

An early employee, Bob Cross, the chief engineer who started in 1935 and helped design the television studios almost 20 years later, recalls numerous events and dignitaries during his employment with both stations until his retirement. Roosevelt, Eddie Cantor, Lou Gehrig, President Dwight D. Eisenhower, and Jean Piccard's Rochester night flight are only a handful of his memories from more than 50 years of broadcast engineering.

Gentling's innovation eventually led to establishing KROC-TV. Plans for television broadcasting began in 1948, six years after his

death, when his widow and son, G. David Gentling, continued his dream. Owing to a halt on TV applications, local management waited for 3.5 years before being granted a construction permit.

Erecting a four-ton, 575-foot tower and a small studio atop Hennessey Hill, three miles west of town, allowed KROC-TV to go on the air July 16, 1953, with a 75-mile radius viewing area.

With 18 people employed full time, everybody played double roles between the two media, including engineer Cross, newscaster Ray Thompson, sportscaster Bernie Lusk, and weatherman Jerry Boyum.

Beginning with one studio camera in a 14- by 24-foot studio, the operation soon added a Quonset building. After the first year the station signed on with NBC's "Today" show at 7 a.m., had a full morning schedule until noon, at which time it signed off until 3 p.m., and then resumed until midnight. Full-day telecasting began in 1958.

KROC Radio studios moved to the new First Avenue Building in downtown Rochester in 1940, and later both the radio and television studios moved to combined quarters at 601 Sixth Avenue South-

Gregory Gentling, founder, president, and general manager of KROC Radio, and Clare Fisher, commander of the William T. McCoy Post of the American Legion, were instrumental in getting President Franklin D. Roosevelt to come to Rochester to present American Legion honors to the Drs. William and Charles Mayo at Soldiers Field in August 1934. Courtesy, Olmsted County Historical Society

west in November 1966.

When Quincy Newspapers, Inc., of Quincy, Illinois, purchased KROC-TV from the Gentling family in July 1976, it remained at the First Avenue Southwest location, and its call letters became KTTC-TV. John Leifheit is the present general manager, and Thomas A. Oakley is president and chief executive officer of Quincy Newspapers, Inc.

At that same time KROC-AM and FM moved to a new location at 122 Fourth Street Southwest, with Gregory Gentling, grandson of the founder, as owner and general manager.

An early photo of the KTTC-TV (then KROC-TV) studio in the Quonset building on Hennessey Hill. At work on a commercial set are (from left) Phoebe Thompson; Bob Heiden, cameraman; and Ray Thompson, news director (at news set). Courtesy, RCA Broadcast News, October 1955

WINONA STATE UNIVERSITY-ROCHESTER CENTER

Pictured at the 1986 dedication ceremony of WSU-Rochester Center's new building on RCC's campus are (from left) Dr. Gerald Christenson, chancellor of the Minnesota State Community College System; Dr. Geraldine Evans, Rochester Community College president; Dr. Thomas Stark, Winona State University president; and Dr. Robert Carothers, chancellor of the Minnesota State University System.

As early as the 1920s, Winona State University offered evening classes in Rochester. Initially its mission there was to further educational opportunities for area teachers. Later, however, nursing classes became another popular offering for Rochester's medical sector.

Through the years programs became more varied. Since 1973 eager residents have attented WSU's expanded degree opportunities for nontraditional, adult students in the evenings and on weekends. In 1982 limited daytime offerings in business, accounting, and psychology began, and more recently, the pursuit of lifelong learning has given impetus to a wider spectrum of course offerings.

During this span of years, classes were held wherever space was available. Dr. Norma Dison, WSU nursing professor, remembers her classes being held at Graham Arena while the ice-making machine was noisily preparing a new surface. Northrup School, Golden Hill School, and Rochester Community College have also been used.

In recent years WSU-Rochester Center has noted a growth at the rate of 15 percent per year, tri-

Many nontraditional students seek lifelong learning opportunities at Winona State University-Rochester Center.

pling its size since 1977.

Such growth laid the groundwork for WSU's special partnership with RCC, the 2+2 relationship. Through the close, working alliance of faculty and administration of the two educational institutions, RCC's lower-division and WSU's upper-division courses are dovetailed for smooth, cost-effective, and complete degree programs in numerous areas of study. So unique is this concept that it is the first time the Minnesota state legislature has provided for a state university to build on a community college campus.

A whole new meaning to this

principle took shape physically when construction of WSU's new $2.9-million facility on RCC's campus began in the fall of 1985. The attractive complex of nearly 30,000 square feet houses a computer center, a complete nursing department, all administrative functions, 17 classrooms, expanded student services, and additional resident faculty. In addition, WSU will be installing an interactive television system, which will enable classes to be held simultaneously in Winona and Rochester.

Offering more than 225 courses each year, WSU serves approximately 1,000 students every quarter. It is projected that the new center will be servicing increasing numbers through 1990.

According to Dr. Leon Zabrowski, Winona State University-Rochester Center director, and Beryl Byman, WSU director of community relations and development, "To indicate how much we have grown, 14 undergraduate degree programs are now offered jointly between RCC and WSU. Moreover, with approximately one-third of WSU-Rochester Center's student body in the graduate program, three master's degree programs are also offered."

Looking to the future, Winona State University-Rochester Center continues to respond to the demand for quality, affordable education for southeastern Minnesota's residents. It is committed to preserving and extending knowledge in its new academic setting.

ROCHESTER COMMUNITY COLLEGE

Rochester Community College, founded in 1915, has played a major role in education for the Rochester area. It was established by Dr. Charles H. Mayo's motion at an August 1915 school board meeting that provision be made to add two years of university work to the high school curriculum. The Rochester Board of Education, of which he was a member, voted unanimously for its adoption, and H.A. Johnson, superintendent of Rochester Public Schools, was authorized to hire faculty for initial course offerings.

Opening for classes on September 14, 1915, Rochester Junior College had four faculty members, including its first dean, W.G. Bolcolm, and 17 students enrolled in six classes of language, history, science, and mathematics.

Although under the supervision of the University of Minnesota, it was part of the local school system and, therefore, located in a few rooms on the fourth floor of the Coffman Building on Second Street Southwest. Other high school classrooms, laboratories, and service areas were used jointly by the high school and college.

It was not until June 2, 1923, that Rochester Junior College held its annual commencement—up to that time graduation exercises were incorporated with Rochester High School's ceremony. That commencement also marked the beginning of granting the Associate of Arts degree.

That same year enrollment topped the 100 mark; 10 years later it reached 200; yet, not for another 20 years would it reach 300. It was not until after World War II that increased enrollment required Coffman's entire third and fourth floors, and soon the entire building, plus leased space in the Midway Building, the YWCA, the Armory, Rochester Public Library, and various other public structures.

In 1965, when Rochester State Junior College celebrated its 50th anniversary, a staff of 56 and an enrollment of 1,695 students, representing 31 states and nations, were indicative of its growth and commitment to education.

Control of the college passed from the local school board to the Minnesota State Junior College Board in 1964, when the state legislature created the community college system. One year later the legislature transferred approximately 115 acres of state-owned land used by Rochester State Hospital near Horse Thief Cave on Highway 14 East for a new campus. With more land acquired in 1967, and after 51 years in the Coffman Building, the new, $1.8-million multi-building campus was begun for 1968 fall quarter occupancy.

Today, with more than 12 buildings on its wooded site, more than 3,400 students currently enrolled, approximately 100 full-time and numerous part-time faculty, a support staff exceeding 65, and the new 2+2 arrangement with Winona State University-Rochester Center, RCC looks forward to celebrating its 75th anniversary in 1990.

Noteworthy, too, is that, having graduated in excess of 13,000 students in its 74 years, one of Rochester Community College's former honor graduates, Dr. Geraldine Evans, is currently its president.

Rochester Community College moved to its present campus on the southeast edge of Rochester in 1968. Established in 1915, the college has graduated well over 10,000 students.

THE KAHLER CORPORATION

As times change, so do business directions and the economy, but the Kahler Corporation, with Harold "Hal" Milner at the company's helm since 1985, is a viable force in the lodging industry in Rochester and throughout the United States. With lodging as the main thrust over the past four years, Kahler's scope has broadened with acquisition of hotels and resorts in Denver, Colorado; Fort Worth, Texas; Salt Lake City, Utah; Chandler, Arizona; Morgantown, West Virginia; and Wisconsin Dells, Wisconsin.

Today The Kahler Corporation is forging ahead to the twenty-first century with its expansion programs. Certainly the newly

opened 194-room Kahler Plaza Hotel is a fine tribute to John Kahler, whose caring and business insight made its mark on Rochester's history.

Armed with determination, boundless ambition, and innovative ideas, John Kahler came to Rochester in 1896 to manage the 45-room Cook Hotel. Now, nearly a century later, The Kahler Corporation continues to serve its lodging guests and Rochester area resi-

dents with its founder's standard of excellence and caring.

Within five years after Kahler's arrival, his simple business code of providing warm hospitality and the best of service reversed the failing Cook's situation.

At the request of the Mayo brothers, who wanted him to establish a hotel for patients and their families, he bought the 30-year-old E.A. Knowlton home on Second Avenue Southwest, the Damon Parkade's present location. Opening in 1907, the structure became the first Kahler Hotel and the first Kahler hospital-convalescent facility. It was the first facility of this kind in the world.

Within six years Kahler added two wings to his new hotel. In its 140 rooms the hotel included an obstetrical and surgical hospital unit on the third floor and later incorporated headquarters for the Kahler School of Nursing. It was renamed the Damon Hotel, the maiden name of Mrs. W.J. Mayo, in 1921 when Kahler built his new Kahler Hotel.

In that span of 25 years, increasing numbers of patients necessitated more hospital, convalescent, and hotel facilities. In 1912 the Zumbro Hotel, which also had an operating room and patient rooms, opened. An eight-story addition completed five years later provided supplementary space for medical offices and laboratories.

Allied services were also in demand. Laundry services, nurses' training programs and dormitories, diet kitchens, and other patient support facilities were necessary. It was imperative that lodging and allied interests be consolidated. As a result, John H. Kahler became president of the newly formed Kahler-Roberts Corporation in 1917. It was renamed The Kahler Corporation two years later.

BELOW: In this 1921 photo, construction of the "new" Kahler Hotel is well under way. Additions were built in 1954 and 1968.

RIGHT: John H. Kahler founded The Kahler Corporation.

Harold Milner, current president and chief executive officer of Kahler Corporation. Courtesy, Potter's Photography

By 1919 Rochester's population of 15,000 handled more than 60,000 clinic patients annually. Kahler built, expanded, bought, sold, and renamed numerous convalescent-hotel complexes, among them the Stanley and Rochester hotels, and the original Colonial, which opened in 1915 as a two-wing hotel. Patient needs demanded it be converted to a hospital. Likewise, the Worrall Hospital, intended for use as a nurses' dormitory, was converted to a hospital, with wings added also.

Following World War I the continuing demand for rooms and services led to the establishment of the new Kahler Hotel and Hospital, opened in 1921 with Mayo personnel staffing the hospital and Kahler providing nursing services. In reality it was the culmination of John Kahler's inventive mind.

This unique triple-plan facility incorporated a 210-bed hospital with three operating suites and laboratories, a 150-bed convalescent unit, and a 220-bed hotel with its top four floors devoted to hospital patient care. An added convenience to the patients, their families, and the medical personnel was the subway connecting the Kahler and Zumbro hotel-hospitals to the Mayo Clinic.

The Tudor Gothic structure's exterior was handsome, but its richly carved interior woods, cathedral arches, stained-glass windows, chandeliers, and furnishings were elegantly designed. It was considered one of Minnesota's grand hotels.

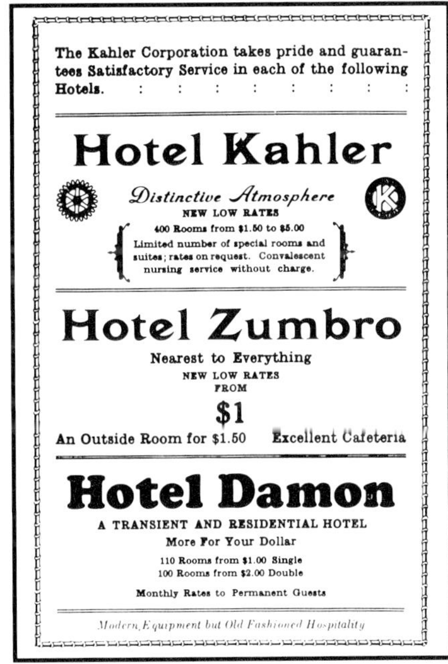

An early Kahler Corporation placard (circa 1922) publicized its hotels' room rates and special features to Rochester visitors seeking lodging.

Related to increased hospital-convalescent needs was another problem area, that of a nursing shortage. With World War I demanding nursing personnel, Rochester's expanding medical facilities also required additional nurses. The Kahler Corporation established the Colonial Hospital Training School of Nurses in 1918, and it had 35 students enrolled in its first class. Beginning with a one-year program, it expanded training to a three-year program by 1920 and continued as the Kahler School of Nursing until 1954, when it merged with the Methodist Board of Homes and Hospitals.

It was in that year, too, when Internal Revenue Service rules became more complex about profit and nonprofit associations being housed under the same roof, that Kahler sold its hospital properties and focused on the lodging business. A 257-room north wing was added to the 1921 structure in 1954; other areas of the ornate original facility were remodeled and refurbished; and the Kahler became a full-service hotel.

Other investments became diversified. Its initial 1908 Model Laundry operation became a major arena of activity, today handling 40,000 to 50,000 pieces of laundry daily. It services the Kahler properties, Mayo Clinic, several hospitals, nurses' dormitories, and other Rochester and southeastern Minnesota lodging facilities.

It purchased several southeastern Minnesota laundries and dry-cleaning properties through the years and is now known as Textile Care Services Division, which currently handles 8 million pounds of laundry annually. It boasts the largest continuous batch washer (where laundry goes in soiled and comes out clean and dried) in the world. That same service also supplies commercial and industrial rental uniforms to various businesses Kahler serves.

Still another branch to that division is Anderson's Formal Wear, Inc., one of the nation's largest wholesalers of men's formal wear. Warehouses in Rochester; Kansas City; Denver, Colorado; Dallas, Texas; and Oakland, California, service retail formal shops with rental apparel.

MARIGOLD FOODS, INC.

While the name Marigold Dairies, Inc., only goes back to 1928, the firm has had a long and distinguished history since 1902.

John Cottrell, co-proprietor of Gem's Restaurant in 1897, later produced ice cream in a remodeled basement until he sold that venture to James Friary in 1905. Under Friary's ownership the business prospered, necessitating expansion in 1911 into new facilities at Broadway and Fourth Street Northeast, the present Marigold location.

W.L. Parkin and Henry Dlouhy purchased the business shortly thereafter, Parkin later buying Dlouhy's interest and the firm becoming the Parkin Ice Cream Company, the largest ice cream producer outside the Twin Cities and Duluth.

Expanding to include additional dairy products, this reorganized firm merged with three major ice cream companies and dairies from the Twin Cities and Wisconsin and became Marigold Dairies, Inc., with E.O. Hanson as Rochester's first general manager and vice-president.

By 1957 diversification provided customers not only ice cream but also milk, butter, cheese, and related dairy items. Yogurt and other cultured foods did not become popular for another 20 years.

Today, well surpassing 80 years of quality ice cream making, employing more than 300 people, producing 20 million gallons of ice cream per year in more than 30 fla-

Marigold Foods, Inc., at its 406 North Broadway location in 1931. Courtesy, Olmsted County Historical Society

vors, and shipping its products to 10 states under the Kemps and Quality-Checkd labels, as well as under major supermarkets' individual labels, Marigold Foods, Inc., is proud of its heritage and its superior products.

Hilda Wood, standing right, worked as a waitress at the Metropolitan Hotel where lunch cost 50 cents to 75 cents. Lunch, or dinner as it was called, included soup, roast beef or roast pork, celery, choice of vegetable, and homemade pie. Lodging at the hotel cost $1 per night. Courtesy, Hilda Wood

PATRONS

The following individuals, companies, and organizations have made a valuable commitment to the quality of this publication. Windsor Publications and the Rochester Area Chamber of Commerce gratefully acknowledge their participation in *Rochester: City of the Prairie.*

Barlow Foods, Inc.
Alvin E. Benike Construction, Inc.
Clements Chevrolet-Cadillac-Subaru Company
Express Services, Temporary and Permanent Personnel, and Robert William James & Associates
Fiksdal Flowers
IBM Rochester
The Johnson Company
The Kahler Corporation
K&K Realty of Rochester, Inc.
KTTC-TV & KROC Radio
Madonna Towers, Inc.
Marigold Foods, Inc.
Mayo Clinic
MEPC Apache Properties, Inc.
PACE Dairy Foods Company, Inc.
Rochester Community College
Schmidt Printing Inc.
Weis Companies
Winona State University-Rochester Center

Partners in Progress of *Rochester: City of the Prairie.* The histories of these companies and organizations appear in Chapter 8, beginning on page 109.

SELECT BIBLIOGRAPHY

BOOKS AND ARTICLES

Andrews, C.C., ed. *Minnesota in the Civil and Indian Wars, 1861-1865.* St. Paul: The Pioneer Press Company, 1899.

Annual Report. Waters Instruments, Inc., 1987.

Baihly, W. Lee. "Vying for Readership: A History of the Rochester Newspapers: 1857-1900." Original research paper, n.d.

Bear, Joseph A., comp. *The Ordinances of the City of Rochester.* Rochester, Minn.: The Post and Record Print Shop, 1901.

Bierbaum, Sherry. *Program for Limited English Proficient Students.* In-house report. Rochester, Minn.: Independent School District 535, 1987.

————. Speech presented to the Refugee Mental Health Workshop on November 19, 1987.

Blegen, Theodore C. *Minnesota: A History of the State.* Minneapolis: University of Minnesota Press, 1963.

Brewer, Nicholas R. *Trails of a Paintbrush.* Boston: The Christopher Publishing House, 1938.

Buckeye Cookery, with Hints on Practical Housekeeping. Minneapolis: Buckeye Publishing Company, 1883.

Callahan, Barbara. "The Doctors Mayo and the Sisters." *Hospital Progress.* July 1965.

"Chateau Theatre." *The Olmsted County Historian,* Vol. 6, No. 1, Spring 1979.

Clapesattle, Helen. *The Doctors Mayo.* Minneapolis: University of Minnesota Press, 1941.

"The Court House of Olmsted County." Typewritten document on file at Olmsted County Historical Society.

Dabney, C. Michael. "Telemedicine—the Link That Binds." *Mayo Alumnus,* Winter 1987.

Division of Publications, Mayo Clinic. *Sketch of the History of the Mayo Clinic and the Mayo Foundation.* Philadelphia: W.B. Saunders Company, 1926.

Erickson, Kelly Carper. "Worrall Hospital, 1919-1967." *Rochester Methodist Hospital Chronolith,* Autumn 1987.

Gernes, William D. "The Stoppel Farm: A Historic Resource." Article on file at the Olmsted County Historical Society.

Granahan, David. Personal letter to Doris Blinks, librarian/archivist, Olmsted County Historical Society, December 9, 1978.

Gregg, O.C., ed. *Minnesota Farmers Institute.* Minneapolis: Tribune Job Printing Co., 1896.

Harwick, Harry J. *Forty-Four Years with the Mayo Clinic: 1908-1952.* Rochester, Minn.: Whiting Press, 1957.

Heilbron, Bertha L. *Documentary Panorama.* St. Paul: Minnesota Historical Society, 1949.

"Heinie, the Bell Ringer of Central School." Typewritten document on file at the Olmsted County Historical Society.

Herrick, Lucy Stewart. "History of the Monday Club of Rochester." Handwritten document on file at Olmsted County Historical Society.

Hill, W.H., ed. *History of Olmsted County, Minnesota.* Chicago: H.H. Hill and Company, Publishers, 1883.

History of the Minnesota Horticultural Society, from the First Meeting Held at Rochester in 1886, to the Last at Saint Paul in 1973. Saint Paul, Minn.: Office of the St. Paul Press Company, 1873.

Holland, Newton. *Rochester Art Center: The First Annual Report of the President.* November 11, 1947.

Holmes, William. *Dedicated to Excellence: The Rochester Methodist Hospital Story.* Rochester, Minn.: Rochester Methodist Hospital Foundation, 1984.

Holmquist, June Drenning, ed. *They Chose Minnesota: A Survey of the State's Ethnic Groups.* St. Paul: Minnesota Historical Society Press, 1981.

Howard, George F. "Visiting Day." *Olmsted County Teacher,* February 1903.

IBM Rochester Site Communications Services. *25th Anniversary. IBM Rochester.* July 25, 1981.

Independent School District 535. *Community Education: Comprehensive Plan 1987-1988.*

Jerabek, Esther. "Minnesota: Melting Pot of Many Peoples." *Gopher Historian,* Spring 1967.

Johnson, Paul C. *Farm Inventions in the Making of America.* Des Moines: Wallace-Homestead Book Company, 1976.

The Legislative Manual of the State of Minnesota. St. Paul: The Pioneer Press Company, 1901.

Lettermann, Edward J. *Farming In Early Minnesota.* St. Paul: Ramsay County Historical Society, 1978.

Loeffler, Robert J. "Visits of Circuses to the City of the Doctors Mayo." Research paper on file at Olmsted County Historical Society.

Maloney, Mrs. William Brown. "Mrs. Mayo, Wilderness Mother." *The Delineator,* September 1914.

Mayo, Louise W. Letter to Carrie France, December 4, n.d.

Mayo, W.J. "The Work of Dr. Henry S. Plummer." *Proceedings of the Staff of the Mayo Clinic,* Vol. 13, No. 27, July 6, 1938.

"Mayo One Earning Its Wings in Rural Areas." *Mayovox,* September 1987.

McKinley, Marvin. *Wheels of Farm Progress.* St. Joseph, Minn.: American Society of Agricultural Engineers, 1980.

McNamara, Brooks. *Step Right Up: An Illustrated History of the American Medicine Show.* Garden City, New York: Doubleday & Company, Inc., 1976.

Mills, Robert K., ed. *Implement & Tractor: Reflections on 100 Years of Farm*

Equipment. Overland Park, Kansas: Intertec Publishing Corp., 1986.

Mitchell, W.H. *History of the County of Olmsted.* Rochester, Minn.: Shaver & Eaton, 1866.

Native American Center of Southeast Minnesota. *Traditional PowWow Intertribal Program.* April 1987.

Nelson, Clark. "Mayo Roots." *Mayo Clinic Student/Faculty Newsletter,* October 28, 1987.

"Olmsted County Fair Dates Back to 1860." *Agri News,* August 5, 1976.

Olmsted County, Minnesota, and Its Advantages of Soil, Climate and Location, with Rochester as a Most Favorable Point for Manufacturing. Rochester, Minn.: Post Steam Newspaper, Book and Job Printing Office, 1884.

Premium List and Rules of the First Annual Exhibition of the Southern Minnesota Poultry and Pet Stock Association. Rochester, Minn.: Post Steam Printing House, 1884.

Robinson, Edward Van Dyke. *Early Economic Conditions and the Development of Agriculture in Minnesota.* Minneapolis: University of Minnesota, 1915.

Rochester Business & Normal College. *Rochester Business & Normal College Catalog.* N.p., 1905.

"Rochester Dairy Cooperative." Typewritten document on file at Olmsted County Historical Society.

Rochester International Association. *RIA: Unity in Diversity.* Brochure. N.p., n.d.

Rochester Seminary. *The Rochester Seminary Gazette,* Fall 1865.

Saint Mary's Hospital. *School of Nursing. Saint Mary's Hospital.* N.p., 1924.

Schelbecker, John. *Whereby We Thrive: A History of American Farming, 1607-1972.* Ames, Iowa: Iowa State University Press, 1972.

Schlitgus, Ernest H. "The Dubuque Trail." *Olmsted County Historical Society Monthly Bulletin,* February 1960.

Scott, Roy Vernon. "Pioneering in Agricultural Extension: Oren C. Gregg and Farmers' Institutes." *Minnesota History,* March 1960.

Severson, Harold. *Rochester: Mecca for Millions.* Rochester, Minn.: Marquette Bank & Trust Company, 1979.

Smith, Eleanor. *50 Years: Serving Humanity through Education.* Rochester, Minn.: Methodist-Kahler School of Nursing, 1968.

A Souvenir of Saint Mary's Hospital. Rochester, Minn.: Saint Marys Hospital, 1922.

State of Minnesota. *Laws Of Minnesota Relating to the Public Schools and the State Normal Schools.* St. Peter, Minn.: J.K. Moore, State Printer, 1881.

Stefferied, Alfred, ed. *The Yearbook Of Agriculture: 1943-1947.* Washington, D.C.: U.S. Government Printing Office, 1947.

Stoppel, Beverly and Gerald. "The Stoppel Family." Typewritten document on file at Olmsted County Historical Society.

Taylor, Dr. David V. "Committees of One: The Black Experience in Minnesota." Study guide for film.

Ullman, Mrs. Joseph. "Saint Paul Forty Years Ago: A Personal Reminiscence." Typewritten document on file at Olmsted County Historical Society.

U.S. Department of the Army, St. Paul District, Corps of Engineers. *Revised Final Environmental Impact Statement: Flood Control and Related Purposes, South Fork Zumbro River Watershed, Rochester, Olmsted County, Minnesota, St. Paul.* U.S. Post Office and Custom House, August 1977.

Walters, Phoebe Mayo. "My Father and I." *The Mayo Alumnus,* Vol. 13, No. 4, October 1977

Waters, G.M. Business memorandum. November 6, 1952.

Waters, Thomas F. *The Streams and Rivers of Minnesota.* Minneapolis: University of Minnesota, 1977.

Wechsler, Charles A. "The Winged Giants of Silver Lake." *The Minnesota Volunteer,* January/February 1979.

Wilder, Lucy. *The Mayo Clinic.* Minneapolis: The McGill Lithograph Co., 1936.

NEWSPAPERS

The following newspapers were used extensively in the research for the text. Individual articles are too numerous to list.

Daily Post and Record
Olmsted County Democrat
Record & Union
Rochester City Post
Rochester Daily Post
Rochester Post
Rochester Post-Bulletin

INDEX